The Deepest Secrets of Dark Psychology

Become That Person Who Controls Every Situation. Discover How to Mold People's Decisions in Your Favor and Shape Your Path by Mastering Manipulation

Table of Contents

Chapter 1: Introduction to Dark Psychology 5
    Persuasion 10
    Manipulation 11
    Deception 11
    Subliminal Messages 12
    NLP – Neuro-Linguistic Programming 15

Chapter 2: Body Language and Lies 17
    Body Language 17
    Deception 21
    The Deception Spectrum 22
    Deceptive Topics 24
    Deceptive Tactics 26

Chapter 3: NLP 30
    NLP: A Brief History 36
    The Pillars Of Nlp: How To Apply The Knowledge In This Guide 37
    NLP Presuppositions 38

Chapter 4: Psychology Of Influence, Persuasion And Manipulation 52

Chapter 5: Brainwash and Hypnotism 62
    Hypnotism Is Real 62
    Hypnotic Tactics 63
    Brainwashing 71

Brainwashing Contexts 72
The Process Of Brainwashing 74
The Impact Of Brainwashing 78
Conclusion **80**

Chapter 1: Introduction to Dark Psychology

It's a bit of a well-kept secret that the ability to manipulate people is a useful tool. It's one of the reasons how businessmen and politicians get and hold their positions. There comes a certain point in your life wherein completely turning off your emotions and being pragmatic is a skill you need to have. Nobody likes to discuss it because we have this societal fear of the reality that people can just be seen as a means to an end.

The late Steve Jobs was particularly renowned for his ability to work people's emotions and to say just the right thing that would get them to come around to his view. It was so strong, in fact, that the people around him developed their own term for it: the 'reality distortion field,' a phrase coined from a similar phenomenon in the Star Trek universe.

There are numerous historical instances of Steve Jobs taking advantage of his unique ability to get precisely what he wanted. One such instance was when Jobs, in the 1980s, was trying to get Pepsi CEO John Sculley to come to Apple. This exchange spawned a famous line that many know today: "Do you want to sell sugared water for the rest of your life, or do you want to come with me and change the world?"

There is a lot that can be said about his specific ability to charm and manipulate people, not the least of which was his deep understanding of what people wanted as well as what people wanted to hear. Add on to this an understanding of subtle intimidation, power cues, and a large amount of passion and charisma, and you have a powerhouse who could get pretty much whatever he wanted.

How does all of this apply to you? Well, you're reading this because you want to learn how to work with people from the inside out. You want to know how to say just the right thing to get what you need and how to manipulate people such that you can bypass any obstacles, so they will do exactly what you want. If that's the case, then you've come to the right place.

The fact is that the mind is a relatively simple thing. While the brain is infinitely complex, the manifestations of the conscious mind are both resolute and easy to work with. Most people work in very obvious and predictable ways such that if they're a 'normal' person, you can rather easily figure out the best way to work with them in no time flat.

The purpose is to analyze all of these patterns within the context of people in general so that you can learn the best way to put these trends to use. Some people will, of course, break these 'standard' molds, and for this reason there are a couple chapters dedicated to the idea of knowing the person you're working with, reading their inner and outer body language and mental cues, and knowing how to build a paradigm that you can easily manipulate them with.

In the end, this is about using the concept of neuro-linguistic programming to its fullest to get what you want out of people. A more common term for this is 'manipulation.' However, the aim of neuro-linguistic programming is slightly different. Neuro-linguistic programming is more focused on the long-term shifting of attitudes where manipulation is more based on immediate gains. That isn't to say that neuro-linguistic programming isn't a form of manipulation though, it absolutely is.

When you hear the term 'manipulation,' you will probably have some sort of knee-jerk reaction like, "Wait, isn't manipulation wrong?" And to this question, there is no simple answer.

I have to say no, though. Manipulation isn't wrong, manipulation is simply a tool. How you use it can determine whether it's wrong or not. For example, an example of manipulation being objectively wrong is doing something that gets somebody terribly hurt. There are also some unspoken rules that you should never break. For example, while it's pretty easy to take advantage of the fact that somebody's parent is dying, actually doing so is a major ethical gray area.

If you stick to maintaining an ethical approach, then manipulation actually proves itself as a method of understanding people and knowing how to work with them so things will work out better for you. You can even use manipulation for good purposes. One such example is Steve Jobs yet again, who used his reality distortion field for good causes, such as when he would convince his employees that it was possible to do something that was more or less impossible, which in turn, would make them work harder for the end result and eventually lead to a new mark being set in technology.

We all know that psychology is the study and analysis of the human mind and human behavior. So, what is Dark Psychology? It is the science and art of manipulating and controlling the human mind through various methods. Psychology is central to human interactions, thoughts, and actions whereas Dark Psychology involves the use of tactics of persuasion, motivation, coercion, and manipulation to get what you want.

There is a phenomenon in this realm referred to as the Dark Psychology Triad that consists of elements that help in detecting potential criminal behavior in people. The Dark Triad is a combination of traits including Narcissism, Machiavellianism, and Psychopathy. What are the characteristic features of each of these Dark Triad traits?

- Narcissism – is related to lack of empathy, high levels of egotism, and grandiosity

- Machiavellianism – People with this attitude have little or no sense of morality and ruthlessly employ manipulation and other tactics to exploit and/or deceive others.

- Psychopathy – These people come across as very charming and charismatic and deep down are highly impulsive, selfish, lack empathy, and are fairly remorseless.

Yes, it is true that none of us wants to be manipulated and yet it happens in our daily lives with unerring regularity, many times unwittingly. Additionally, we also use mind control and manipulation tactics to try and get what we want. Dark Psychology involves studying the psychodynamics of people who prey on and victimize others to achieve their own ends.

There are people who use dark psychology tactics knowingly and with the intention to cause harm to others and there are those who use or are prey to these tactics in unwitting ways. Moreover, it is a survival instinct in all living beings to be wary of our surroundings and use guile and deception to survive and thrive. There are multiple studies that prove this innate ability to victimize others.

Although we believe that we have control over our actions and reactions, under extreme pressure, it is very difficult to predict our behaviors and there are high chances that many employ dark tactics to escape from these pressures. The following studies are examples of how human minds behave in unpredictable ways when compelled or sometimes even when it may not have needed such an extreme reaction.

Let us look at some of these experiments conducted in the '60s and '70s by psychologists. While there are controversies surrounding the experiments and plausible rationalizations were provided in retrospect, it goes without doubt that the human mind can be very unpredictable and is capable of reaching out to its dark aspects with little or no provocation.

The 'learner' was actually only an actor.

If the learner gave a wrong answer, the volunteers were told to give electric shocks by turning the 'dial', which had labels ranging from mild pain to extreme pain to even fatal. The experimenter wearing a lab coat told the volunteers that they should continue to increase the intensity of the 'electric shock' until the right answer was given by the learner. The volunteers could hear the simulated screams of the learner from the other room. If the volunteer did not want to increase the intensity, then the experiment told them to continue employing the following statements:

- Please continue

- The experiment needs you to go on

- It is essential that you go on

- You have no choice; you have to go on

There were startling and disturbing outcomes from this rather controversial experiment. Despite hearing the simulated screams of extreme pain from the 'learners,' 65% of the volunteers turned the knob to 'fatal.' They did not even bother to ask about the health of the learner. Yet, most of the volunteers said that they would have never behaved this way but did not find the wherewithal to stand up to a figure of authority (lab-coated experimenter). Dark Psychology is easy to trigger, isn't it?

The most disturbing observation of these kinds of experiments was the fact that the volunteers were not even aware that they were being manipulated and that they were delving into the dark aspects of their minds. Another study which proved the unconscious behavior under authority goes as follows:

A group of volunteers was asked to watch a screen in which a basketball game was going on. They were told to count the number of passes that took place between players wearing white shirts. At some point during the game, a person dressed in a gorilla costume walked into the court. The participants were so engrossed in counting the number of passes that they did not even notice this aberration. In fact, many participants swore that no such disturbance took place! They were unconsciously following the orders of the experimenter.

Another common dark psychology tactic is called 'priming' in which people's behaviors can be changed without them even realizing it. For example, read this sentence, 'The house was so old that it groaned, creaked, and struggled to stand on its shaky foundation.' Now, suppose you were to stand up, chances are very high that you will unconsciously have taken care to do so at a slower pace than usual as you were just now 'primed' for old age.

Politicians are known to use priming to change voting preferences based on the location of the booth. Like this, there are many studies which prove that accessing and employing the dark side of our minds is not just easy but can happen without us even being aware of it.

Moreover, these theories have been applied and checked repeatedly throughout the history of mankind and dark psychology is an integral part of our minds. This is not the same as conspiracy theories. Dark psychology only represents the innate need and desire for man to dominate over others who are weaker than himself so as to achieve his own ends. Marketing advertisements are classic examples of manipulating the minds of the buyers and convincing them to buy the product, which they may or may not need.

Therefore, it makes sense to know, understand, and appreciate this aspect of our minds and use strategies and tips to 'prime' our minds and those of others in ways that will result in win-win situations for all concerned stakeholders.

Persuasion

Persuasion is one of the most popular forms of mind control. This method is used in so many different areas of life that many people don't even recognize when it is happening. That is exactly why it works.

Persuasion is not the same as convincing, although most people believe the two are the same thing. However, persuasion is the act of skillfully encouraging someone to do what you want them to do without them realizing you're doing it, whereas convincing someone means that you are using tactics that are easy to recognize. To explain it a bit further, persuading means to skillfully present facts and information in a way that doesn't make it obvious that you are doing so, and encouraging people to do what you desire for them to do. Convincing people, on the other hand, is very obvious and often includes a lot of back-and-forth and ultimately nagging, begging, or pleading someone to make the decision you want them to make after they have already chosen the alternative.

When you are learning about persuasion, it may seem easy. In reality, it is a strategy that requires a lot of time, effort, and practice. You cannot simply read about persuasion and then run out and master it. Instead, you really need to ensure that you grasp the concept and that you practice putting it into action in your daily life. In chapter 6 you will learn about many real-life strategies that can help you further integrate this technique into your life.

Manipulation

Manipulation tends to be regarded as one of the darker methods of mind control, and many people think it is a nasty thing to do. However, when you learn to use manipulation properly, you can use it to gain control over virtually anyone's mind and have your desired effect on their decisions and actions.

Unlike persuasion, which is typically comprised of conversational tactics, manipulation involves external influences to help encourage people to do what you want them to do. These include strategies like building trust, and proving why they should do what you want them to do. While some of these strategies are conversational, they are often impacted by external influences unlike persuasion which relies merely on wording structure and methods of structuring your sentences and conversations.

Deception

Deception is an extremely sophisticated strategy that is used in mind control. This is not the process of outright lying to people, but rather tactfully covering up certain pieces of information to avoid them from ever being discovered. This strategy allows people to knowingly omit information from conversations without being considered liars since they have never directly been asked, and therefore they have never directly lied.

When you are partaking in deception, you have to be tactful and consistent in keeping the conversation away from any question that may put you in a position where you must either come clean or actually lie. Using deception as a secondary manipulation method for mind control purposes means controlling the conversation and preventing it from ever going in the direction that would suggest information that you are lying or covering up information.

In order to skillfully use deception, you need to know how to guide the conversation in a way that leads the listener to believe something without ever actually being told to believe it. For example, if you want to prevent someone from finding out that you are attracted to someone they also like, you could create the illusion that you are not. You never actually admit that you aren't, you just lead the conversation so that it can be assumed that you aren't.

This is a powerful form of mind control because it allows you to deny ever doing anything wrong. Since you have never admitted to anything or lied about anything, you can easily say that it was the listeners fault for not asking, or for assuming anything was implied.

Subliminal Messages

When you use subliminal messages, you are sending messages without someone actually knowing that you are doing so. These messages tend to slip past the conscious mind and directly into the subconscious. The powerful thing about subliminal messages is that you can be telling someone one thing, and yet having them hear something entirely different. While this conscious mind digests something that they are willingly accepting, their subconscious mind may be hearing something entirely different. Because you have put them into a receptive mode, they are more likely to react and respond in the way that you want them to, and their subconscious mind is more likely to accept the information as well.

Subliminal messaging is powerful because it allows you to control the mind without any indication that you are doing so. You can speak directly through the conscious mind and into the subconscious mind, thus planting information, evidence, and knowledge into the subconscious that encourages your listener to support your position and act or think in the way that you want them to. You are literally programming their mind with your desired messages, and they have no idea that you are doing so.

Mind control is a very powerful strategy that can enable you to have people thinking in your favor. These individuals are going to unknowingly be listening extremely closely to your sentences and hanging on your every word, while giving into anything you want. Because of your masterful ability to control their minds without them even knowing it, you will be able to have any desired outcome effortlessly.

People often have a few different traits which you can use to understand them. Things such as their body language, their life situation, and their emotions. All of these impact one another. In the following chapters, we will break down all of these aspects to help you understand exactly what position you're in.

Body language is a huge giveaway about what's going on in a person's head. Understand that in terms of neuro-linguistic programming, body language is a language in and of itself.

We're going to expand on this concept just a bit so we can gain an understanding of how we can read and process other people's emotions.

This is actually a very critical part of neuro-linguistic programming, and one of the things that makes it such a challenge. Doing it properly is not like picking a lock. There is no 'correct' path for you to do it right. It's a very dynamic activity, which is heavily centered on your ability to understand what the other person is thinking in a very concrete manner.

Understand that a person has many physical tells, but that's not the be-all-end-all of what is going on in a person's mind. Some people are so good at hiding their emotions that you can't really tell what's going on under the hood unless you know them very well.

Often, people will have two emotions running in parallel. These can be difficult to decipher, but generally, they have the emotion at their foreground — this is what they display themselves to be feeling — and they have their emotion in the background, which is what they are feeling under the hood.

Some people are worse than others when it comes to hiding their emotions while some people make no effort at all. There are times, too, where these emotions may run in tandem and are exactly the same.

The truth is, though, that if you're trying to convince somebody of something, you always have to consider the possibility that people don't often feel what they're projecting themselves to be feeling. Usually, you have to consider what these parallel emotions could be.

We'll focus more on the underlying emotions when we get to the chapter on psychoanalysis. However, for now, we just need to focus primarily on reading emotions on the surface.

People convey a lot of their emotions through their body language as well as through their tone of voice and their choice of words.

If you pay attention to a person's eyes, you can read a lot into somebody's foreground emotion. While, hopefully, you're emotionally competent enough to read foreground emotions relatively well, note that some of these can be difficult to break apart from one another. For example, while the difference between annoyance and anger are slight in terms of their physical display, they have far different emotional connotations. Annoyance is much shorter and less severe, though perhaps more immediately snappy. Anger is more brooding and harder to work your way out of.

Their tone of voice will also tell you a lot. Often, when people aren't being completely honest about the emotion they're presenting, their voice will sound ever so slightly off. Being able to recognize this and using context clues to figure out what's really bothering them or going on in their head is very important.

Sometimes their choice of words will give you hints as well. Pay attention and try to notice if their sentences are structured differently. Are they shorter? Is their choice of words more serious than usual?

In essence, pay attention to a person's body language, as it will tell you a lot about what you need to know when it comes to what a person is feeling, at least on the surface level. When you combine that with your analysis of their underlying conditions, you actually get a very potent piece of information that you can work with.

NLP – Neuro-Linguistic Programming

NLP involves the three most powerful elements that contribute to the human experience and they are; neurology, language, and programming. So, how can we use NLP to influence people? Here are some answers to that.

NLP techniques are in use both in businesses and personal relationships to influence people around you. NLP techniques are designed to help you get your message across in the correct way so that they are interpreted by the people to give you your desired outcomes. NLP techniques also focus on the choice and appropriate use of language to help you motivate people around you to get something good done.

NLP techniques are designed in such a way that if used correctly, they can help you teach others how to become more productive and efficient in their lives which, in turn, helps you in your life as well. NLP techniques are also designed for salespeople so that they are able to reach the subconscious levels of the buyers' minds in such a way that they feel good and happy about buying the product or service.

The basic presumption of NLP is that each of us is unique in the way we think, we interpret, and the way we present ourselves to the outside world. NLP says that if we know how we think, then we can be empowered to change the way we think. Extending the same logic outside of us, if we know how people think, we can empower ourselves and them to influence changes in their thought processes.

Let us take an example. Each of us has a unique way of translating what we see around us into thoughts. Our preference could be to the use of sight, sound or touch or a unique combination of all three. If our preferred sense is that of sight, then we easily convert the events in our life into pictures and images in our thoughts. If our preferred sense is that of touch, we easily convert our experiences into feelings.

Let's take this a bit further. Suppose you had a preference for the sense of sight. This preferred sense is actually very evident in the way you interact with others. For example, you will use phrases like, 'See you later,' or 'I can see how this will turn out,' etc. You will normally be the type of person who decides that when something or someone is out of sight, then that person or thing is out of your mind too.

So, with a person whose sense preference is that of touch, phrases such as 'Catch you later,' or 'I'm getting a bad feeling from this,' etc. will be used. So, by knowing these preferences and the way they become evident through their language and thought, we can understand people better and once we understand their behavior, we can more easily influence the way they think.

It is a natural thing to be fond of those individuals who are like us in the way they think and behave. So, by knowing their preferred means of communication, we can use the same way to communicate with them and therefore make it easy for us to influence them.

A classic example of NLP influencing technique is to synchronize your breathing with that of the other person. Watch when the person breathes in and you match your inhalation with that. When you match every breath of yours with the other person's, you will find an invisible connection to the individual giving you a great boost in terms of influencing his or her thoughts.

Chapter 2: Body Language and Lies

Body Language

Humans are adept at reading body language or the nonverbal signals we use to communicate. These nonverbal cues can communicate more information that the words we choose. From facial expressions to how we stand, the things we don't say convey volumes of information.

People have a natural inclination to engage in helping behavior. Our communal nature makes it imperative to understand the meaning behind nonverbal cues. This makes every person on earth a mind reader. It just so happens that some people are better at it than others.

Our communities aren't a big homogenous mass though. We divide up into micro and macro groups and prioritize our "tribe" when making decisions. In the long run, it provides significant benefits to team up rather than every person for themselves.

But our mind-reading abilities add a layer of complexity. Humans can lie or otherwise hide their true intentions. This often provides a significant short-term advantage at the cost of ill will from others in the community.

Deception is an active performance. It requires decent brain power and effort to maintain a ruse for any length of time. We can only focus on a few things at a time so our body language often gives away our true thoughts and intentions.

I have learned a few tricks that can help anyone improve their ability to influence others through body language. They are simple but have helped everyone from vacuum salesmen to Ted Bundy hide their true intentions.

These techniques aren't going to stop racism, misogyny or ass-hats. But they can pressure others to respond in subtle or overt ways. With enough practice and proper execution, they will push people over the fence of suspicion and help you change a no into a yes.

Practice Perfect Posture: When I walk into a room, people immediately know that I am the one in charge. I don't have to tell them I'm in charge, they have already decided I am before I even open my mouth. I communicate this information to them primarily through posture.

Posture communicates our status within a group more than the clothes on our back and the words coming from our mouths. It only takes a second for someone to start making decisions about me. So I make sure to instantly communicate authority and power through the way I hold my body.

I stand and gesture using specific techniques that subtly show dominance and control without seeming like a tyrant or manipulative. These techniques include standing erect, using gestures with palms facing down, and with filling my space.

The brain is programmed to equate power with the amount of space they take up. Standing straight makes you look taller and holding the shoulders back maximizes the space I take up. But if I slouched, I appear project submission and weakness.

Maintaining good posture helps others understand that I am someone worth knowing. While using my space to make broad and expansive gestures shows others I know my limits. These combine to command respect and help others to value engaging with me.

Adopt a Likable Tone: Coming into an interaction defensively or acting like I want to fight is naturally off-putting. It sets me up to be rejected and makes the other person retract. If my intention is to influence a subject, I need them open and welcoming, not closed and defensive.

So I approach them as an old friend, helping them relax slightly and naturally open up. By showing I am comfortable, it signals to others that they should be as well. It's surprising how welcoming people can be when they relax a bit.

By acting friendly and open, they almost instinctively respond with warmth. They may remain suspicious of your intentions if you overplay it though. So be friendly, not fake, and believe that people want to help.

Example: When I meet someone for the first time, I smile and introduce myself in a familiar way and ask something about them. I begin my encounter on the basis that we are old friends meeting again. This helps me with the next trick...

Mirror Body Language: One of the most important elements of attraction is believing that the other person understands you on a deep level. The feeling of someone just getting you is intoxicating. The more we feel they understand us the deeper our connection.

It's important to emphasize commonalities rather than differences. The more we have in common, the more likely we are to align our motives and goals. These situations show us that the other person is similar to us. Since body language communicates the most information in the shortest time, it's the best way to establish that feeling of similarity.

People naturally mirror body language. We often don't think about our stance, tone, and position in conversation consciously. By monitoring and mirroring the other person's body language, it sets them up to be more attracted to me and value my opinion higher.

Example: Be subtle! If the other person shifts their weight to lean against a wall, lean up against it too. If they talk with their hands, I make sure to gesture when I talk. If they cross their legs, I do the same but in a slightly different position. I don't make huge changes, just enough to be in sync with the other person.

Establish Control: Once we are in sync, I begin to lead the conversation. I continually build rapport and when the time is right I begin changing my body language to encourage them to mirror me. Once they follow my lead, I know that I am in control and can diffuse an intense situation or build excitement.

The fastest way to gain trust is to mirror the other person's body language. Before I start leading, I have to get them to be in sync with me. The better I can do at mirroring and tone, the faster they sync up and I gain control of the conversation.

Questions help establish control of a conversation. It may seem counter-intuitive, but the person giving answers is weaker than the person asking the questions. So I ask questions as often as possible, although I rarely give the other person time to answer them.

Once in control, I can lead the conversation where I want. All the while I watch and study their reactions. I keep tailoring my questions and responses to encourage the other person to respond emotionally. The more emotion I can work up, the more control I have.

Example: If I want to convince a person to sign a contract, I control the conversation by asking questions and mirroring their body language. I'll cross my legs if they cross theirs and make similar gestures as my subject. Once their body language starts syncing up with mine, I ask questions like, "What are you going to do once you sign?" and "I can't believe we managed to get these terms. You must feel pretty lucky right?"

Make Eye Contact: We are the only primates in the world with white in our eyes. That's because we use them as a primary way to communicate. The eye is called the window to the soul because of how integral it is to body language.

Without good eye contact, people will perceive you as nervous, shifty, or unattractive. Making eye contact with someone creates an intense connection. That connection is integral to appearing trustworthy and engaged.

This doesn't mean to stare people down. Eyes can communicate aggression as easily as timidity. Refusing to break eye contact can make others uncomfortable and appear overly intense.

Example: I maintain eye contact for about 80% of my interactions. When the other person is talking, I maintain eye contact unless they are talking about something in eyesight or are becoming overly excited. I lower my eyes to communicate sadness, raise them for praise and keep my eyes mainly on the speaker.

Give Good Face: When talking about body language, we tend to focus on the torso and limbs. Things like posture, where and when to touch someone and how to hold our hands dominate the conversation. We often underestimate the power of emotive expressions.

It always surprises me how effective a smile is in communicating emotions. It can indicate pleasure, happiness, irony, appeasement, or a superiority complex. A genuine smile is one of the most underrated aspects of attraction.

We are the only primates that smile at people we like. The others see it as a threat display. People naturally find a mouth full of pearly white teeth to be very attractive.

Just make sure any smile you give is genuine. When people realize you are faking a smile, it sours their disposition. It gives away that you are deceiving them and calls everything you do and say into question.

Deception

Deception is a key aspect of dark psychology. Like many other dark psychological tactics, it can be difficult to tell whether any given instance of deception is dark or not. Before we explore the difference between dark and normal deception, let's first understand exactly what deception is.

A lot of people would state the viewpoint that lying and deception are the same thing. This is inaccurate. Lying is a form of deception but is by no means the only form deception can take. Rather than thinking of deception as "lies" it is better to think of it as "misleading." Any action or word capable of making someone believe something other than the truth can be accurately termed deception.

So what are some common manifestations of deception? Lying, omitting the truth, implying falsehood or fraudulently providing evidence for something false are all examples of deception. You will probably realize that you have done some of these things at some point yourself. Does that mean that all acts of deception are examples of dark psychology? Not at all.

Everyone deceives to some extent or another. People might deceive others for a range of reasons such as kindness, embarrassment or feelings of inadequacy. For example, studies have shown that many, even most men will lie about their height on dating websites. This does not make them practitioners of dark psychology! People even deceive themselves about a range of issues including their health, ambition, and happiness. Such regular, day-to-day examples of deception do not equate to dark deception. So what does?

Deception can be seen as dark when it is carried out with either a negative or indifferent intention toward the person being deceived. Normal deception is usually motivated by an inability to face up to the truth in one way or another. Dark deception, on the other hand, is an understanding that the truth does not serve the deceptive aims of the deceiver. Therefore, the truth is either changed, hidden, or ignored in favor of a version of events that better suits the purpose of the person deceiving.

Put simply, people who deploy dark psychology use deception to harm, not help. They help their own interests, but at any cost, regardless of who gets hurt.

Some people assume that if a deception is small scale it cannot be seen as dark, whereas larger deceptions must be inherently dark. This is not the case. By exploring the idea of the deception spectrum you will see that it is not the size of a deception that determines whether it is dark or not, rather the purpose behind the deception.

The Deception Spectrum

To understand the idea of deception it is important to understand that it can occur on either a large or a small scale. One of the main mistakes that people often make is assuming that deception is only serious if it is big and does not matter if it is small. This is a grave error. Small deceptions can be used in a powerfully dark way by skilled manipulators and are often more effective than large deceptions. Similarly, some of the largest deceptions ever carried out have been performed by deliberate manipulators to serve their own aims and objectives. Dark examples of various types of deception, large and small, will now be presented to illustrate the idea of the deception spectrum.

So what are some of the ways that smaller deceptions can be used by people who practice the art of dark psychology? Often, small deceptions are used initially to test the victim's gullibility and condition them into believing the deceptive statements and actions of the manipulator. If people are conditioned to believe a range of smaller lies over time, they are more likely to believe a larger lie in the future. This gradual conditioning is not the only way smaller deceptions can be used as a dark psychological weapon.

Smaller deceptions can also be carried out to undermine a victim's trust in their own powers of logic and reason. If a manipulator deceives a victim over small issues, and the victim begins to question what is happening, the victim may well conclude that their suspicion is irrational and they therefore cannot trust their own judgment. Most people are more likely to conclude that their own judgment is faulty, rather than another person is deceiving them over seemingly small issues. Users of dark psychology are aware of this general "trust" that people have and seek to exploit it without mercy.

Large-scale deception can also be an example of dark psychology in practice. One of the largest deceptions possible is to convince someone that you are a different person than you say you are. Not in terms of personality or some other detail. An entire identity. Name, date of birth, everything! The most skilled users of dark psychology are able to persuade other people to buy in entirely into their portrayal of a false identity and background.

Now that it has been shown how manipulative users of dark psychology are able to use the deception spectrum for their own aims, we will explore some of the most common topics and subjects that people are deceived about. We will then look at exactly how these large- and small-scale deceptions are carried out by exploring the specific tactics that are used.

Deceptive Topics

Everyone has heard the old saying that "money is the root of all evil." This is an exaggeration, but money is certainly the route of many deceptions. Deception and money can cross paths in many different ways. Some people deceive to attain money, others deceive to hide their own money, or lack thereof. Because money is such a common topic, some of its deceptive uses will now be explored.

One of the most common dark psychology deceptions involving money is carried out by the professional beggar. These are individuals that aim to extract money from the public despite having plenty of it. These beggars draw on a number of dark psychological principles to get money from innocent victims. Such beggars have been known to inflict injuries upon their own body to appear more desperate to victims. Some of the most extreme deceivers in this area have even turned their own children into heroin addicts to use them as part of their scam. This is an example of the depths that money-related deception can sink to.

Marital status is another common area where people choose to deceive. Sometimes, people try and hide their married background to seduce a new victim. This can be for either financial or sexual or other reasons. Some people have multiple wives spread out across the world who do not know about each other. This type of deception has become harder with the advent of the Internet and the ability to check up on people via social media. The best deceivers are able to hide their tracks expertly and keep each fraudulent wife separate from the next.

Some people choose to appear falsely married when they are in fact not! This type of deception can occur for several reasons. A married couple is often perceived as more trustworthy than a couple that is not married. Some users of dark psychology are aware of this perception and use it for their own schemes and plans. Some people pretend to be married for reasons related to tax and insurance. One of the most common deceptions of this type is the creation of a fictional dead husband or wife to gain people's sympathy and, often, their money as a result.

A criminal background is another area of life many people are deceptive about. This is because it is almost impossible to be trusted professionally or personally if you have committed certain crimes. For example, if a man meets a woman, and the man has committed a serious crime in his past, how likely is he to tell the woman he has just met about this? It seems doubtful that he would be entirely upfront. Interestingly, such deception is not always dark. If the man does it through fear of being rejected, this is not dark deception. If he does it with the intention of hiding the truth to later harm his new victim, then this is a clear indication of dark psychology at work.

One of the most evil and deplorable examples of deception related to criminality is when someone who has committed serious past offences, such as rape, hides these in order to commit similar actions in the future. People with a dark psyche of this type are often compelled by their abnormal urges to the point they will do literally anything to hide the truth and carry on giving in to their compulsions.

Manipulators also feel that deception is a great way to hide any abnormal or socially unacceptable feelings they have. This stops their victim from being alerted to the kind of person they really are until it is too late. For example, if someone who uses dark psychology is interested in a person only for sex, they know this focus is likely to be a red flag to their victim and will therefore deceive their victim. They may either overtly lie or imply that their true intention is love and commitment. The victim falls for the deception, the manipulator's exploitation is complete and yet another person is hurt by deception.

One of the most common areas to be deceptive in is the truth of a manipulator's personal feelings for a victim. Deception is the most powerful tool the manipulator has to influence a victim to perceive things in the way the manipulator wishes, rather than how they really are. Typically, deception will be used in relation to interpersonal feelings to portray the manipulator as something they are not. Some of the most common examples of this use of deception will now be provided.

Within the field of romantic relationships, deception is often used to mask the manipulator's true intentions. Deceptive words and actions will leave a victim feeling as if the manipulator "just happens to be" what they are looking for at that particular time in their life. In actual fact, skilled manipulators are able to identify vulnerable people and probe their psychological needs and weak points. This information can then be used to deceptively cloak the manipulator and make them appear to be something they are not, but something the victim wishes they were. This deception is often the starting point of more complex, long-term manipulations.

Deception can also be used to soften up the victims' feelings in a non-romantic context and increase their susceptibility to manipulation. If, for example, a manipulator is looking for a vulnerable person to use dark psychology against, they may initially portray their own intentions as innocent. Even if the intention is to become intensely close to a person, the manipulator will usually deceptively portray himself as a very casual, easy-going person. This deception can be prolonged if needed. The manipulator will be whatever the victim needs, for as long as the victim needs, in order to get their guard down and allow the thorough manipulation to begin.

Deceptive Tactics

You now understand what exactly dark deception is, its spectrum and the common areas people are deceived about. Now it is time to examine closely the specific tactics used by manipulators to darkly deceive. Each of the tactics is equally powerful and careful manipulators know exactly how to use each at its most impactful and harmful time. It is important to note that manipulators will not neatly alternate between the four following categories—any given deception is likely to involve a blend of each.

Lying is perhaps the most obvious and common form of dark deception. It is likely to be chosen as a technique when the manipulator has decided that their victim is susceptible to lies and unable to gauge the truth. This may be because the victim is a generally trusting person or that the manipulator has carefully worked on their target over time to lower their guard. If a manipulator has chosen to deceive through the use of lies then it is likely they have also thought of a way to hide their lies and explain any discrepancies the victim may notice. Manipulators are masters of having a "plan b" at any given time during their dark deception.

Deception through lying is likely to occur in a subtle and thought out way. A skilled deceiver is likely to embed their lie into truthful information over time. For example, a manipulator will probably tell a story that is 90% true and 10% false. The victim will perceive the story as entirely true and not have any way of separating and ascertaining the truth regarding the deceptive 10%. Some manipulators also spend time associating truth with a particular tone of voice or gesture. They can then say something falsely deceptive in this tone of voice, or with this gesture, and it is likely to be perceived as true by their victim's subconscious.

Implying is a more subtle form of deception than out and out lying. Implying involves suggesting something false is true rather than boldly stating it is. Let's illustrate this idea with an example. If someone wanted to deceive a victim about the amount of money they have then they could either lie or imply. A lie would sound something like "Oh I'm a successful guy. I've made a lot of money," while the manipulator is well aware this is not the case. An implication may take the form of "it's so stressful trying to handle things with my accountant. Trying to get my tax bill down takes a lot of my time." The manipulator has acted and spoken in a way that implies they are wealthy without flatly stating it.

Manipulators often favor implications, such as those just mentioned, as they provide plausible deniability. If the victim accuses the manipulator of lying, the manipulator can say they did no such thing, and technically be truthful. Implications are also powerful if a victim happens to have an active imagination. The deceptive implication can be seen as a seed planted in the mind of the victim. The victim's own imagination then does the manipulator's work for them and fills in the blank spaces to create an idealized version of reality, according to the manipulator's prompts.

Omission is a failure to mention something that is true. This stands in contrast with other forms of deception such as lies or implications. Both lies and implications use falsehood to cover truth, to varying degrees. Omission instead goes the route of simply ignoring the truth and leading the victim's attention away from it. For example, if a manipulative user of dark psychology had an aspect of their past they did not want their victim to focus on, they would simply never mention it. They would draw attention to other times in their past or swerve the subject whenever possible.

One way omission is often carried out is by creating an "emotional fence" around a situation. This is a tactic in which a manipulator implies that a particular period of their life, or topic, is too painful or uncomfortable to discuss. The victim will then avoid talking about this time, or asking awkward questions, of their own volition. If the victim does bring up the subject the manipulator wishes to avoid then the manipulator can play the "it's too painful" card. This allows them to avoid the truth while making the victim feel guilty for touching on a "painful topic"!

Fraud is the most elaborate and criminal form of deception used by those who deploy dark psychology. Think of fraud as a lie on steroids. Instead of simply lying about something from their past, a fraudulent dark deceiver will have false documents, stories, and other evidence to back up their lie. The most skillful deceivers will use such things in a subtle way. Rather than saying, "no, I really am a Doctor, look at my certificate!" they are likely to make subtle displays such as leaving the fraudulent evidence around for their victims to see for themselves. Deceivers know that if they are too "pushy" with their fraudulent claims then the victim will intuit that something is wrong.

Worryingly, fraud is more common than ever thanks to the prevalence of computers and the Internet. Deceivers are able to use professional-grade software to quickly and easily make realistic-looking documents of almost any type. Such frauds can be carried out for either personal or professional reasons. Some of the most serious types of professional fraud include instances where people have obtained jobs using a false identity, stolen from a company, and then disappeared before their identity can ever be known. Personal frauds include terrifying tales such as people with HIV spreading the disease with the help of falsely produced certificates of clean sexual health.

When dark deception enters the realm of fraudulence it is a sign that the deceiver is a dangerous and committed user of dark psychology. For a person to risk running afoul of the law and facing serious criminal charges, they have to be truly committed to the manipulation they are attempting. If many users of dark deception are amateurs, the deceptive fraudsters are the dangerous professionals that must be avoided at all costs.

Ironically, one of the main ways dark deception is often carried out effectively is following the manipulator's own pantomime of feeling deceived by their victim! Many manipulators know that, by portraying their victim as the deceptive party, they are able to deflect any attention away from their own deceptive efforts. This is an example of a deception within a deception and shows the complex, layered approach to manipulation that many deceivers use.

Chapter 3: NLP

Neuro-linguistic programming (NLP) is an approach to communication, personal development, and psychotherapy created by Richard Bandler and John Grinder in California in the 1970s that leverages the power of language to influence thought.

NLP has infiltrated every element of modern business life. Everyone in sales or marketing has practiced these methods to some degree, but psychoanalysts and occult leaders around the world give it a bad name.

Most people don't grasp the underlying principles and struggle to apply them in everyday environments.

But some skilled individuals can harness this power to give them an unbeatable advantage. The techniques are best used in a one-on-one or small group environment. The fewer people involved, the easier it is to read and apply NLP methods.

NLP is a complex subject and is often taught over the course of years. That's because it takes practice to learn the range of reactions people can express. But the promise of learning people's inner secrets makes this technique especially attractive to con artists and law enforcement.

NLP is basically a method of reading a person to understand their personality and individual quirks. NLP users watch for subtle cues that are invisible to most people and use them to control a conversation and the emotions of the people in it. Eye movement, skin flush, pupil dilation, and nervous tics all provide information.

After an initial round of observation, skilled users can mimic their subject in subtle but impactful ways. The NLP user thus opens their target to suggestion and steers them toward an intended destination.

A skilled NLP user can determine:

Which side of the brain their subject uses

People fall along a spectrum between creative and analytical. New science shows that brain function is actually distributed across the brain. But it is still helpful to think of people through this lens.

Word choice, sentence structure, and associations all reveal details about the person that uses them. I begin by looking at what my target is saying and how they present their points, then I adjust my words to be more analytical or emotional based on my subject.

Left-brained people often use words that elicit emotion or experiences. Right-brained people like to include things outside their experience or expertise.

Example: Left-brained people: "That looks fun. I bet we can squeeze in!" Right-brained people: "Is that safe? Is it rated for someone my size?"

Which sense is most important to them

We have more than the five senses (sight, sound, taste, touch, and smell) most people know about. We also have a sense of order, balance, morality and a host of others, and each of us has one or two that are more important than the rest.

I listen to see which sense is most important to my target. Then I use some of the same words they did in my reply.

Example: If vision is important to my subject, I say things like, "Do you see what I'm saying?" Audio-focused people respond better to "Can you hear where I'm coming from?" Meanwhile, I might ask a taste-oriented individual to "savor that for a moment."

How their brain stores information.

Our brains are the most complex computers we have ever come across. They store and process billions of bits of information a second. Each one functions a little differently. One of the biggest areas of divergence is in how people store information.

Some individuals have a memory like a sponge, soaking up everything near them. Others are more like a strainer that catches big chunks and allows everything to pass through. NLP techniques help people discern the difference and to what degree.

Over time, NLP users get better at keeping track of information. With enough time, users can improve their information tracking abilities to near-genius levels. This gives us an advantage over anyone who isn't as experienced or naturally gifted.

I use this information to determine how much info I need to overwhelm my subject. If I want to lose them in the details, I simply include more than they can keep straight. If I want them to follow along, I keep the details and figures to a minimum.

Example: I will occasionally remember something wrong on purpose. It's best with something small like a phone number or address. If my subject corrects me, I can see how well they store information. The average person can only hold seven numbers in their head at once so it normally only takes me asking for them to remember two phone numbers to see where they fall along the spectrum.

When they are lying or making things up.

People perform specific behaviors when they make things up called "tells." NLP users like me can pick up on these tells and be able to call out the liar as they lie. Some people are better than others at lying but everyone has at least one tell.

Skilled liars understand that for someone else to believe their lie, so must they. So they convince themselves of it first. They often don't display all the signs of dishonesty because they truly believe the lie as they tell it.

Practice can help people fall for their own lie but the process demands a selective memory. This feature is more reliably detected than the oft-cited slight downward glance. It also proves to be a more consistent indicator of ingrained deception than awkward looks. Power imbalances also make a refusal to make eye contact less reliable as well.

Example: When my best friend (let's call him Ted) won't look me in the eye during his story. He keeps looking down and to one side of me, then the other. Another person (let's call him Fred) tells his story without looking away at all.

When Ted looks away I become suspicious, but Fred's refusal to lock away is also a red flag. If they are subjects, I cut them some slack. As long as they don't change demeanor mid-story I can attribute some of it to simple nervousness.

How to make someone drop their guard.

NLP users like myself leverage these techniques to convince others that I am just like them. People can't help but like someone they recognize as a kindred spirit. So I combine the techniques above to highlight our similarities.

The more alike we are, the more a subject likes me. So I listen intently to what they are saying. Then I respond to them with the signals that I know appeal to their inner selves. This encourages my subjects to reveal more about themselves to me willingly.

When someone likes you, they want to include you in their lives. Listening to what they say often provides deep insight into what controls their lives. People offer up their darkest secrets willingly, believing that I truly understand them.

So you can condition people without their consent/knowledge.

Let's face it, people don't like finding out someone was manipulating them. It violates the idea that we are in control of our lives. But sometimes the truth is hard to take, and we need someone to help us see the way without calling us out on it.

We all manipulate those around us to one degree or another. This can be as simple as breaking a bad habit or establishing new relationship rules with a toxic family member. By steering them in the right direction, we can help them respond how we prefer.

NLP doesn't brainwash someone (that's covered elsewhere) or cause them to do something out of character. But it does reveal the strings that control each of us. What you do with those strings once you have them is up to you.

Once the subjects are open and receptive, I present my request in terms that they would prefer. I use strong action words with leaders, comforting and kind words with emotionally sensitive subjects, and common words with the less educated. I do everything in my power to appear similar to my subject in thought and deed. This ensures they are the most receptive to my desires and avoids having to issue orders and ultimatums.

Example: When I need a favor, I never ask for it right out the gate. Instead, I begin by building rapport. I ensure my body language is open and tailor my questions and responses to the person I am trying to influence.

Proponents of NLP believe that how you behave has a certain structure to it. Therefore, NLP aims to examine this structure to redefine the way your brain performs and responds to the information it receives. NLP helps you understand the things that make you tick. It opens your eyes to how you perceive the things that happen to you and around you on a daily basis. When you fully understand these things, you can handle situations in a better manner, and communicate more effectively.

Your neurological system is responsible for transmitting all the information your brain receives from your environment. In this context, your environment refers to everything external including all your organs- your ears, your eyes, your skin, stomach, lungs, and every other part of your body.

Your brain processes the information from all these parts of your body and transmits them to your brain and vice versa. For instance, once your brain receives information, it processes it and decides if it is good or bad news, and then transmits it to emotions that could be joy, tears, or laughter.

The takeaway here is that your brain determines how you respond to everything going on around you and how you communicate with others. Now, imagine being able to somehow, alter the way your brain handles this information and force it to react in a certain way. That is the whole logic behind NLP.

NLP helps to change your personal programming (think of computer programming: how programmers can change computer code to get a device or software to perform specific task or behave in a specific manner). It helps you re-organize your internal programming so you achieve the desired results you want.

To frame it in a simpler manner, NLP helps you achieve the following:

1. Increases Your Chances of Success: Generally, life is problematic and your day-to-day life whether at work, with your family or at leisure will be full of challenges. NLP helps you change how you view these challenges as well as your outlook on life. It helps you change the way you see life so that unimportant things stop weighing heavily on, or bothering you. It gives your life a deeper meaning and helps you organize your priorities.

It helps you identify your strengths and weaknesses so you can concentrate on things that can help you become better and more efficient, which helps you become more successful.

2. NLP Improves Your Communication Skills: NLP fosters positive thinking, which makes all your communications positive. It helps you redefine how you think and feel, which makes you a better verbal and non-verbal communicator, which then makes it easier to share your perspective with others and become.

So in essence, NLP helps you to become better at expressing yourself.

3. NLP Synchronizes Your Body and Feelings: When your mind and body are not in harmony, putting your thoughts and plans into action becomes very difficult. However, once you start using NLP, you unify your mind, body, and feelings so you can create a better connection and work towards achieving your goals.

You now have a better understanding of what NLP is and what it can do for you. Before we start using it to reprogram our behavior and maximize our potential, let us delve a bit deeper into its history:

NLP: A Brief History

John Grinder and Richard Bandler founded NLP in the 197o's at the University of Santa Cruz, California. At that time, Richard Bandler was a (AMIS) Information Sciences & Mathematics Master's level student while Dr. John Grinder was a professor of Linguistics.

They both studied people who they believed to be exceptional communicators and very good at helping their clients achieve desired results and necessary change. Particularly, they were interested in finding how it was possible for some people to effectively deal with difficult or sick people, defying the odds where other people have failed.

Grinder and Bandler chose to study three renowned psychotherapists- Virginia Satir, the developer of Conjoint Family Therapy, Fritz Perls, the founder of Gestalt psychology, and Milton Erickson, one of the major contributors to the development of Clinical Hypnotherapy. They also studied the skills of two linguists- Noam Chomsky and Alfred Korzybski, as well as social anthropologists Gregory Bateson and Psychotherapist Paul Watzlawick.

Neuro-Linguistic programming eventually exploded to include other disciplines and spread to several other countries. Unfortunately, in the 198o's, due to some dissatisfaction that Grinder had about some coding work they did together known as the 'classic code,' Blander and Grinder had a falling out. This led to a separation that led Grinder to team up with Judith Delozier to form newer models later named 'The New Code.'

Neuro-Linguistic Programming has come a very long way and many scholars have developed new codes, techniques, and versions, thus making it easier for ordinary folks to apply it in their lives to effect real transformation.

Although originally developed for use in the field of psychotherapy, professionals now apply NLP in all fields including Doctors, Accountants, Engineers, and every other profession in the world; from the way it looks, the future of NLP continues to look bright.

The Pillars Of Nlp: How To Apply The Knowledge In This Guide

To understand how to apply NLP to your personal life, you have to understand the four pillars of NLP. The four pillars of NLP are rapport, sensory awareness, outcome thinking, and behavioral flexibility.

1. Rapport: Rapport refers to how you build and maintain relationships with yourself and other people. Rapport teaches you how to say no to requests and things you do not want while still maintaining a good professional relationship and friendships with the people whose requests you reject.

2. Sensory Awareness: Another pillar of NLP is sensory awareness; sensory awareness teaches you how to pay closer attention to the things going on around you- how to make better use of the senses of sight, sound, touch, hearing, smelling, and taste.

3. Outcome Thinking: When you face a challenge, instead of being stuck, NLP teaches you to focus on what you want and helps you make decisions that will help you achieve these things.

4. Behavioral Flexibility: This refers to how you do things and handle situations. NLP helps you to do things differently. It gives you flexibility and the ability to change a course of action when one course of action leads to failure.

Authors Romilla Ready and Kate Burton describe how the four pillars can translate into your day-to-day life with this interesting illustration.

Imagine you ordered a new software to help you record all the names, addresses, phone numbers, and other important friends and clients' details. After spending time to purchase and install the software, you discover the software does not work because it has a coding bug.

You contact the software company's customer service department and they are rude and unhelpful. At this point, you have to employ your rapport building skills with the customer service manager so they can listen to your complaints. You would need to increase your sensory awareness by listening carefully, controlling your feelings, and deciding on the most suitable response. You have to know the outcome you desire by engaging in discussions with the customer service manager; do you want a refund or a replacement. Lastly, your behavior needs to be flexible enough to accept other outcomes if the desired one is unachievable.

That is how NLP helps you to become a better communicator and helps you achieve the things that you want without a lot of stress or frustration.

NLP Presuppositions

NLP presuppositions are basic generalizations or general beliefs in NLP that can be useful to you when you act as if they are true.

Some common presuppositions of NLP include:

1. The Map is not the Territory: Alfred Korzybski takes credit for this statement. He explains that we experience the world through the human senses of sight, touch, hearing, taste, and smell, which he refers to as 'the territory.' The experiences you get from these senses then transfer to the brain where they make an internal representation that he refers to as 'the map'.

You create an internal map in your brain; your experiences shape this map, but another person who has had the same experiences would never have the same exact internal map like yours (their perceptions and the way their senses perceive information may be different). This simply means that what is outside can never be the same as what is inside your brain.

If you are a doctor, what pills mean to you may be vastly different from what they mean to a patient and even a law enforcement agent.

The point is that we all make different internal representations of the same things depending on our backgrounds and personal contexts.

To be a better communicator and a generally better person, you need to learn how to see things from other people's eyes- try to understand the internal representations or map of the person you are trying to communicate with. Rather than respond negatively to other people's behavior you may deem inappropriate, focus on trying to understand why that person might have behaved that way. This would make you a happier person who accepts people's actions and inactions with greater ease.

2. There is no failure, only feedback: This very important NLP presupposition will help you, but only if you can live by it. There is no one person in the world who does not experience setbacks and failures. It is up to you to choose whether to allow those setbacks to bring you down or you want to take lessons from your setbacks and these lessons as a learning experience that helps you become better at whatever you failed at the first time when you decide to try again.

Whenever you fail at anything, rather than give up, always ask yourself these five questions:

* "What am I trying to achieve?"

* "What have I been able to achieve so far?"

* "What are the things I have learned (feedback)?"

* "How can I use the lessons learned to better my performance?"

* "How am I going to measure my performance and success?"

3. The Meaning of the Communication is the Response it elicits: How the person you are communicating with perceives the information you are trying to pass across is the most important thing. No matter how good your intentions are, your listener interprets information based on how they receive it.

The onus therefore, rests upon you to pass your messages across carefully in the way you want your listener to receive it. Before you start communicating, have a clear understanding of the desired outcome of the conversation, and then carefully construct your conversation to elicit the exact response you want.

4: If What You Are Doing Is Not Working, Do Something Different: This is yet another presupposition and a very simple one at that. Do not be fixated on things that do not work for you, instead, change your tactics.

Determine why what you are doing is not working and what you can do to get better results.

5: You have all the Resources You Need to Create Desired Outcomes: Everyone has what it takes to develop, grow, and become a better version of themselves.

6: People are Much More Than Their Behavior: The fact that a person is behaving badly does not necessarily mean he or she is bad. People behave badly when they do not have the inner resources to behave differently. Most times, helping them change or improve on these resources would help them improve their behavior and start behaving better.

7: Body Language is Important: When communicating, you have to employ the right body language because body language makes up for 55% of how others receive your communication.

For the techniques to work for you, you have to practice them. Most of the techniques listed here are not instant solutions that are going to work in one day; however, with consistent practice, your life would improve and you would get better at what you want to improve.

1st NLP Technique: Setting Personal Anchors

Anchoring focuses on helping you change your state of mind. It can help you stay calm in the face of danger or trouble, and can help you relax and behave in a positive way when people are trying to provoke you.

Anchoring tries to mimic one of Pavlov's experiments. Pavlov experimented with dogs and sounded a bell as the dogs were feeding. Whenever the dogs saw the food and heard the bells, they salivated in anticipation of the meal. After some time, Pavlov began to sound the bell without the food in sight and he noticed that the dogs salivated whenever they heard the bells even without seeing the food.

Anchors are similar; they stimulate a response in your mind and help you control your thoughts and emotions. For instance, rubbing your forehead can be an anchor. Sometimes, anchors can be involuntary. For instance, a familiar smell might bring back a memory from your childhood or a song can trigger a memory of your ex. These are examples of involuntary anchors that work automatically without any self-induced trigger.

Establishing anchors involves producing stimuli when you experience the resourceful state so that the resourceful state pairs with the anchor. Just like with the dogs that begin salivating without a meal in sight simply because they heard a bell, you can establish personal anchors that will trigger a desired response in you whenever you experience anything.

Activating the anchor refers to the act of producing the anchor after you have established it in a bid to trigger the occurrence of the resourceful state.

When you are happy or sad, you are responding to some anchors in your life. When you are feeling motivated and confident or otherwise, you are also responding to some anchors although sometimes, you do not even know what these anchors are. That is why sometimes, you may be in a bad mood without knowing why.

The NLP anchoring technique teaches you how to design personal anchors and use them to produce a desired state of mind. For instance, if you are in an interview situation and you are feeling jittery, but you want to be calm, you can use established anchors to trigger a calm response within yourself. If someone is annoying you, but you do not want to lose your temper, you can use anchors to calm yourself down.

The Resource State

In the last section, we established that we all have the resources we need to achieve the things we desire. Here, the resource state refers to memories of the required state. For instance, if you want to be calm, your resource state here is a memory of a past time where you were calm and relaxed.

The resource state involves striving to make a previous experience vivid so it feels as if you are experiencing it afresh in the present. If you cannot recall a situation where you have felt that way, you can simply just imagine yourself in the resource state.

Types of NLP Anchors

There are three different types of anchors:

1. Visual Anchors: Visual anchors involve using the things you see to provoke a response. For instance, if you want to feel powerful, you can use your wristwatch as an anchor so that any time you want to feel powerful, you simply look at the wristwatch and use it as an anchor; however, the anchor does not have to be objects- you could use people, symbols, drawings, or anything physical as an anchor.

2. Auditory Anchors: Auditory anchors involve using sounds or music as anchors to provoke a response.

3. Kinesthetic Anchors: Touching yourself or imagining someone touching you is an example of a kinesthetic anchor.

How to Set Personal Anchors

To set anchors:

1. Decide the state you wish to anchor (the response you want to elicit e.g. Calmness, happiness, feeling powerful, feeling relaxed, etc.). It is helpful to write down your intention in your journal, so that you can crystalize exactly the feeling or emotion you wish to create a trigger for.

2. Choose the anchor you want to use to trigger that state. You can use a combination of anchors such as visual and auditory anchors.

3. Close your eyes.

4. Tap into your resource state by recalling a memory where you previously experienced the state you want to trigger.

5. As soon as you can vividly recall that experience, activate the anchor (play the music, touch the parts of your body you want to use as anchors, or look at the object you wish to use).

6. Release the anchors as soon as the experience starts to fade away. It is important to release the anchor immediately the experience begins to fade so that you do not anchor a drop in that state rather than the state in itself.

7. Take a break and do something else such as counting from one to ten.

8. Repeat the process from step 1; this time, make the memory more vivid and then try to establish the anchor at the highest point of the experience.

9. Test the anchor to see if the required state occurs. After you have solidified your process, be sure to record everything about your process, to make sure that it is repeatable. What emotions came up during this process? What memories did you specifically trigger? Did you use visual or auditory cues? Write down everything.

10. Check the anchor the next day and continuously until it becomes permanent.

You should always ensure the anchor fires in the same way every time you want to link to the resourceful experience. If you cannot get a desired state when you trigger the anchor, change the anchor to avoid establishing a negative anchor.

2nd NLP Technique: Pattern Interruption

Imagine a situation where you have a favorite route you drive through each time you are going from home to your place of work (every day). This driving pattern becomes repetitive and sometimes, you do not have to place too much effort and concentration into it because well, you already know the drill.

It is kind of like autopilot for you and you take out this time to think of the tasks you need to complete at home, how your day went, and other things while your subconscious takes care of everything else.

Suddenly, you hear a loud sound and bam! A large tree has just fallen and your path is obstructed. You slam the brakes and the car comes to a screeching halt. For the next few seconds, you are sitting in your car wondering what just happened.

Your subconscious is not used to this situation; therefore, it does not know how to respond. At this point, you have to step in; your conscious mind has to take control and issues instructions detailing how to handle the situation. Your subconscious mind is great at running automatic patterns so that your conscious mind can handle other activities that need conscious handling.

When you are trying to alter some patterns, sometimes, automatic habits, thoughts, emotions, and actions can create a problem. It is not as if you are not willing to change, but your subconscious keeps pulling you back, which then cause you to do the same thing repeatedly.

Well, you have to understand that the subconscious mind is very poor at decision-making. Only the conscious mind has the ability to make decisions. As an NLP technique, pattern interruption forces your subconscious mind into a state where it waits for information from your conscious mind.

It helps you break habits and embrace new methods and changes. It helps you re-program your subconscious so that the subconscious becomes a messenger that receives instructions from the conscious mind.

How to Practice the Pattern Interrupt Technique

To practice this NLP technique:

1. Decide on a particular behavior you wish to change. This has to be something you do automatically without thinking about it. For instance, eating junk food whenever you are watching TV could be an example of something you want to change. Write down in detail in your journal exactly what you would like to change.

2. Start observing how the pattern runs. At what point do you start to experience the urge to eat something? At what point do you decide to get up and walk to the fridge? How do you make a choice of what to eat from the different available choices? Record your decision making process in detail in your journal.

3. Create a pattern interrupt completely alien to the behavior you wish to change. For instance, when you experience the urge to eat something, fold some clothes or instead, drink some water. You need to create a pattern interrupt entirely different from the usual pattern. This pattern interrupt has to jolt you just like the tree that fell in front of your car. Again, write down in detail the new behavior you are going to implement.

4. Every time you feel the urge to engage in the pattern you wish to change, use your pattern interrupt to do something else.

Continue to impose this pattern interrupt and before you know it, you will eliminate the habit you want to change and the new habit will replace the old one (as such, the new habit has to be a positive one). You can use pattern interrupt to get rid of addictions and any negative behavior you wish to eliminate from your person. Reflect on the effectiveness of this technique and how it is influencing your behavior.

3rd NLP Technique: The Swish Technique

The Swish NLP technique helps you alter how your memories affect you. It helps you disconnect from powerful negative thoughts that provoke negative feelings that may negatively affect you and your life.

You can use the swish NLP technique to manage your thoughts and feelings especially thoughts and feelings related to the things happening around you. This NLP technique helps you disconnect from past thoughts such as things that irritated you or made you feel embarrassed in the past, present feelings caused by self-undermining thoughts, and anxieties about forthcoming or future situations.

For instance, if due to illness or stress, you take a leave from work and you find yourself worrying about getting back to work, you have an unwanted negative feeling that in this case, is worry. Each time you remember you have to walk into your office when you resume work next week, your stomach churns and your heart starts racing. This means that walking into that office is the trigger.

You have checked this feeling to see if there are any rational reasons for your fear, but there are none because you have checked with your employers and everything is good. Now, you do not want to be worried and afraid whenever you think of walking into your office next week. You want to be confident and enthusiastic about it.

You can use the Swish technique to replace these feelings and change them into positive ones.

How to Use the Swish NLP Technique

To use the swish NLP technique:

1. Identify the feeling you want eliminate.

2. Identify the thoughts or images that provoke the negative feeling.

3. Check if your fears are founded and rational. If they are simply irrational, move on to the next step.

4. Close your eyes.

5. Create a replacement image in your head. This means you should identify how you want to start feeling. It means you should begin to see yourself acting the way you want.

Now, what you want to do is to point your thoughts towards a fresher and more positive direction. The idea is to re-program your brain by changing the trigger so you can know when you should start thinking new thoughts.

6. Think of the trigger image (the negative one) then start inserting the replacement image in between the trigger image. In between worrying, start imagining yourself feeling more confident. Before you begin, write down your replacement image in as much detail as you can, to help you solidify your visualization.

7. Allow the replacement image to become bigger and more vivid so that the trigger image begins a gradual disappearance.

8. Break the state and open your eyes.

9. Start from step 1 and this time, try to insert the replacement faster.

10. Repeat the process about 5-7 times.

11. Test it to see what happens when you try to recall the negative trigger image, you will discover that it becomes more difficult to bring back the negative feeling.

If, however, the negative trigger continues to manifest, the trigger may be more powerful than the Swish technique. In that case, try a stronger technique like the anchoring technique. Reflect on the results of the Swish technique in your journal.

4th NLP Technique: The NLP Framing Technique

The NLP Framing technique draws upon the idea that how you perceive everything depends on your point of view. Framing involves trying to change the meaning you attach to a thing by trying to change its context or setting.

For instance, a person trying to annoy you can seem funny so that, rather than becoming angry, you can start laughing at what the person is doing. The meaning you attach to events and things happening around you is dependent on how you frame it.

You can use your responses and behaviors to change the meaning. Dressing as a skeleton to a Halloween party and dressing the same way to a burial would cast different perceptions even though it is the same costume and the same person wearing it.

NLP reframing helps you change how you see and perceive things happening around you so you can behave in a different way. You can get people to see things differently by reframing events and communication differently to get a different response. By using this technique, you can keep calm in the face of fear and maintain your cool when you should be angry or losing your temper.

How to Use the NLP Framing Technique

To use this NLP technique:

1. First, identify a behavior you consider negative or troubling; a behavior or feeling you would like to eliminate from your persona.

2. Now try to establish a communication with the part creating the behavior or response. This could be a sensation in your body, a picture of another person, a specific sound, or voice: anything that triggers the negative behavior or feeling. Write down both the behavior and any triggers associated with it.

3. Ask yourself what exactly you want- what would you rather feel instead? How would you rather behave? You have to recognize the difference between the feeling/behavior and your intended one.

4. Tap into your creativity to figure out three alternative ways you would rather feel or behave instead of the current negative one or some alternative ways to get your intended outcome.

5. Evaluate your new choices and determine whether they are acceptable or not

6. Check for objections with other parts. Sometimes, when you change an ingrained behavior or pattern, it affects other parts or aspects of your life. You have to ensure your new choices and desired change do not have unintended consequences.

The framing technique helps you tap into your inner resources so you can behave in a way than is far different and superior to your normal way of thinking. Write down any reflections and results from using this technique.

5th NLP Technique: Mirroring and Building Rapport

Mirroring involves mimicking or copying the behavior, body disposition, or speech patterns of a person you are communicating with.

Note: mirroring is very different from aping someone. Aping is where you copy everything someone does; that is not mirroring, that is rude.

Mirroring is subtle and barely noticeable by the person whose body language and speech patterns you are trying to mimic: it has to seem unconscious.

To Mirror someone, you can mimic his or her:

* Speech patterns

* Body language

* Vocabulary style or specific choices of words

* Pace, tempo, pitch, tone, and volume

Mirroring helps you create rapport with the person you are engaging in communication. It makes it possible for the person to warm up to you, trust you, and understand you. A successful interaction can only happen when you maintain rapport with the person you engage in communication with.

There are two approaches to mirroring: you can emphasize the similarities between you and the person, or you can emphasize the differences. Emphasizing the similarities eliminates resistance and antagonism.

Mirroring is a natural thing that most of us do. For instance, if you are trying to talk to a little child, you may crouch so you and the child can be at the same height, or you may talk slowly so the child hears you and understand you better. This is an example of how we naturally mirror others.

How to Practice the NLP Mirroring Technique

To practice mirroring:

1. Mirroring Body Postures: This involves adjusting some parts of your body (or all your body) to match the other person's body posture. Ensure that the posture is a natural one; otherwise, the mirroring may seem disrespectful. You can mirror a person's head and shoulder positions or other natural poses.

2. Mirroring Breathing Patterns: Another thing you can try to match is the breathing pattern. You can mimic the depth or rate of someone's breathing; however, if this breathing is irregular, you should not mimic someone's breathing pattern.

3. Mirroring Voices: You can try to match the voices of those you communicate with by matching the volume, pace, pitch, and choice of words. This can be a very tricky thing to do, but if you learn to do

it subtly, you will be better for it because it will improve your rapport building skills. You do not have to mimic every aspect of a person's speech, but you can speak slowly if the person speaks slowly, or speak in a high tone if the person does so.

4. Mirroring Beliefs and Values: Another way to mimic someone is to try to understand his or her values and believes, and try to see that person's perspective. This is not real mimicry because you do not have to agree with that person's believes and values; you just have to understand him or her and avoid levying judgment. Doing this helps build rapport and makes people more likely to warm up to you.

5. Mirror Language Patterns: You can also mirror a person's language patterns. Marketers and sales representatives commonly use this approach. It makes the person you are communicating with feel understood. What you have to do is to use the same words the person uses or use similar paraphrasing. This ensures the other party feels listened to and understood.

Essentially, mirroring makes the person you are communicating with feel as if you are on the same page. It makes the person feel heard and understood, which ensures the person feels comfortable and at home when conversing with you.

For the next few days, make a habit of mirroring and matching people when communicating. Write down your results and observations. Did it improve your communications? How so?

Chapter 4: Psychology Of Influence, Persuasion And Manipulation

Manipulation literally means using something as a tool to suit your own purposes. The act of manipulating others typically involves using other people as tools. You can't have remorse or shame if you want to be a successful manipulator. You need to view people as pawns that you move around the board game of life. People are very useful; why not use them?

Manipulation has a bad reputation. It's a dark art because it involves making people act against their will or without their knowledge. Nevertheless, this does not mean that manipulation is always used for bad. Sometimes you might use manipulation for positive purposes, such as causing people to make wise decisions. It can benefit the person that you are manipulating as well as yourself. Sometimes manipulation only benefits only you, but it does not harm the other person. You don't have to use manipulation to hurt others, though it is certainly useful in that respect. Manipulation is a valuable skill to possess because it really helps you gain the upper hand and get what you want. It enables you to use people to their full capacity to further your own goals and aspirations.

It is crucial to be sneaky when you manipulate others. People hate being manipulated and made to do things that they do not consent to. But keep in mind that most people have manipulative tendencies and manipulation is far from rare. Therefore, you are not a bad person for using the manipulation tactics included in this chapter. You are simply going after what you want. That makes you powerful and even positive. Just make sure to hide your manipulation attempts and disguise your intentions. Otherwise, people will judge you harshly and get mad at you. You can lose friends left and right if you gain the reputation of a manipulator. We talk more about hiding your manipulative tendencies and actions in Chapter 8 and Chapter 10, but we talk a little about this in this chapter too.

So let's delve into this fascinating and useful subject, shall we?

Make Someone Your Pawn

You can't just manipulate people with whom you don't share a rapport. You have to build a rapport and prime your subject before you can successfully manipulate him. This means that you need to form some sort of relationship with the person. Using a combination of psychological tricks, you can make a person weak for you. Your subject will be willing to do anything for you if you break down his mind and soften him to your attempts at manipulation.

Priming is best achieved through emotional manipulation. You want to play with someone's emotions. The first step is to make someone feel great around you. When someone likes you, he will be more open to your persuasive attempts and will want to please you. He will want to spend time around you because you make him feel good. This time enables you to get your hooks into his mind more successfully. So start with meaningful flattery. Observe your subject to see what means a lot to him. Then compliment him on the things that he values and cares about. For instance, if he loves sports and plays softball on the weekends, talk about sports with him and compliment his pitching techniques or his athletic physique. Over time, he will become increasingly attached to you.

Next, start the emotional roller coaster. As you get to know this person better and make him feel more and more attached to you, start to make him doubt his self-esteem. You can do this by finding things that he is guilty about, or making him feel guilty about things that he does. Always play the victim and make him feel like a terrible person. It's possible to pout like a child but it's even better to act like an adult and pretend to get very hurt about small things he does while telling him that you forgive him. You will look better if you pretend to be an adult who always takes the high road. He will become even more infatuated with you and may start to admire you.

Guilt is very powerful. But so is self-doubt. Plant seeds of doubt in his mind so that he feels insecure. Make him start to hate his friends and family by telling him about horrible things they do or say so that he doubts his social support network and his value to other people. Cause him to question his abilities and skills by saying things like, "You know that you're not good at that!" or "That's not one of your strengths." Tell him that you are simply opening his eyes to his inabilities so that you can protect him from the pain of failure or the pain of being around his hurtful loved ones. Then follow each little insult up with compliments. This will make him very confused. He will start to doubt himself and he will believe what you say because he is attached to you. People are quite sensitive to suggestion, so this method works incredibly well. Meanwhile, he still feels like you are a nice person who cares about him. He won't be ready to end all contact with you just because you insult him from time to time.

You also want to provide him with multiple rewards for what he does for you. When he pleases you, show it and lavish him with praise or favors. Also do favors for him and provide him with lots of services or support so that he is more open to doing favors for you. This is the basic principle of reciprocity, where people like to return kindness and favors that others do for them. You can use the things that you do for him as a bargaining tool. Call on him to return a favor sometime, and he will likely be willing to reciprocate. If he is not willing, guilt him by reminding him of a favor you did for him a while back.

The final part of priming is making someone doubt his sanity and perception. Tell him how he is wrong and come up with convincing arguments as to why. Inform him that he is making things up or misremembering things all of the time. Over time, this will chip away at his security and certainty in his own mind. This method is known as gaslighting, and it is one of the best ways that you can prime someone. Don't take gaslighting lightly. You can use it to totally drive someone crazy over time. It's actually a great form of psychological warfare against someone close to you.

Even if you care about someone, you can still prime him without hurting him. Make him dependent on you so that he never leaves your side. You don't have to be romantically linked to someone to accomplish this sort of dependency. Just offer him something that he can't get anywhere else. Make yourself very useful to him and bolster his ego so that he relies on you for his happiness, convenience, or even financial stability. Disable his other forms of support so that you become the only person in his life. You don't necessarily need to use gaslighting, guilt trips, and other such methods to hurt him; being nice is enough to gain a foothold on someone for persuasive methods. As a friend, lover, or even co-worker, you can accomplish this priming at varying levels. You can do it lightly to someone whom you want to manipulate only slightly. Or you can do it very heavily to someone whom you want to use for life.

Get a Good Read on Someone

There is another side to priming that you really need to take into account. This side is reading. To manipulate someone, you must get a good read on someone. Natural manipulators are adept at reading people at a glance. If you are not so good at reading people right off the bat, then you can use time and priming to get a good read on your subject.

Basically, you want to get to know the person very well. Listen to everything he tells you and glean his speech for potential emotional weapons to use against him. Anything he confides in you or accidentally reveals to you can be turned into a weapon at any time. Save these weapons in your back pocket for when you need to use them.

What are the best emotional weapons? Guilt is probably the most powerful one of all. People hate feeling guilty. So find out things that he feels guilty about.

Also find out things that he loves or cherishes. You can give him these things to make him happy and reward him for his work for you. Or you can cripple him by destroying these things. Love and passion give people power and a will to live. Taking these things away can crush a person. Try to become the gatekeeper of the things that he loves so that you can gain ultimate power over him. For example, bar his access to his loved ones and pitch a fit when he talks to people that you don't approve of, but let him talk to the people he loves whenever he does what you want.

Another way to use what someone loves against him is to trivialize things that he cares about. If he says how much he loves a dish, tell him how it is really not that good. Ruin the small things that he loves. Then you can move on to bigger things. Also, trivialize his opinions. All people love and value their own opinions and believe that they are right. If you make him feel stupid for having certain opinions, then you will be able to chip down his self-esteem and make him doubt his rightness. Make him feel small by trivializing him in every way possible. Eventually, he will come around to your way of thinking and will love only the things that you love because you have made him abandon all that he loves. You will make him feel small and stupid so he will look to you for validation and approval in order to repair his damaged ego.

Trust is a great weapon that you can use. Most people desire to be trusted. You can tell him that he is not trustworthy because of various things that he has admitted to. Then make him do what you want for the sake of winning your trust. Let's say you're dating a guy and you want to manipulate him. Tell him that you don't trust him because he admitted to cheating on his ex. Tell him that you worry he will cheat on you. Or claim that you have been cheated on, so now you have trust issues. This way, he will want to win your trust. He will jump through hoops to make you trust him, including cutting off people you don't like in his life. You can make him cut off female friends and friends who encourage him to drink and have a good time without you around by saying that you feel threatened by these people.

You can also use his reputation to manipulate him. He wants to be liked by others, so you can use that as a weapon. Tell him, "If you do that, everyone at work will hate you. You don't want that, right?" Most likely, if he's a normal person, he will agree that he wants people to like him so he will reconsider doing anything that might damage his reputation. Encourage him to do things by saying that it will gain him favor with different key people. One great way to manipulate co-workers is to give them "tips" on how to please the boss and possibly earn raises or promotions.

Insecurities are fantastic weapons. Whatever hurts him will become apparent rather quickly as you get to know him. Some people are so obvious about their insecurities that you will be able to read what they hate about themselves right away. When someone becomes quiet after a certain subject is brought up, you can bet that he feels insecure about that subject. You can also guess what bothers him based on blatant flaws that he has, such as excessive weight or a poor relationship with his wife. But mainly, you will learn his insecurities by listening to him. Listen to what he talks about and notice the things that seem to bother him or that he complains about. These insecurities are things that you can bring up at opportune moments to hurt him. You can also urge him to do things to atone for what he lacks, or to fix a flaw that he perceives in himself. In addition, you can plant new insecurities in his mind by casually mentioning flaws that you notice in him or saying nasty things to him about himself during arguments.

Finally, his level of affection or even love for you is a powerful weapon. This is why friends or lovers will say things like, "If you really love me, you won't do this." This is also why people like to threaten to leave. You can threaten to withdraw your love from him to goad him into action.

Play the Victim

Playing the victim is your number one "get out of jail free" card in life. If you become adept at playing the victim, you can pretty much justify anything that you do and make your subject feel terrible about anything that he does.

First of all, you want to believe that you are the victim. You can accomplish this by rationalizing things. Use your conscious processes to justify your actions. Think of ways that others have wronged you in order to excuse your actions. As long as you believe that you are the victim, then you won't feel guilty about playing the victim card.

You also want to establish your innocence and vulnerability. You want to appear like an innocent victim being harmed by life so that others feel sorry for you. Tell people sob stories about how the world is against you. Make sure that your situations are not self-imposed so that others don't get irritated and think that you just blame others for your own problems. A good example of this is talking about how you were abused as a child so that you can explain why you have difficulties picking good love partners and healthy friends now. This excuses your actions and makes you seem like a victim who cannot control your own mind or help yourself. Strike sympathy in others so that people want to support you.

When your subject does anything that you don't like, play the victim card. Show him how deeply he has hurt you. You won't accomplish this by pouting, giving him the silent treatment, or throwing a wild tantrum. You will enjoy way more success playing the victim card if you appear mature and calm about something. Inform him in a steady voice that he has hurt you. Offer him consequences for his actions that he won't like. Say that you feel the need to protect your heart and your interests from him. Also, make him feel like a monster by continuing to appear like a saint who never does any wrong. You don't want to do something wrong to him that he can use as a weapon against you when you play the victim card.

Let's revisit cheating in a romantic partnership. If you want to prevent him from cheating, you can play the victim card when he talks to or looks at other women. But be very cautious that you never do anything with another person that makes you look bad. If you do cheat, make sure that he never, ever even suspects you of what you did. Never let him access texts or social media posts that he can use against you, or your whole victim plan will fall apart.

You can also very effectively play the victim card by telling other people what he does to you. Act as if you aren't complaining about him. Just casually mention things that he does that are abhorrent. Blow what he did out of proportion to make him seem terrible, but don't make it obvious that you are trying to complain about him. Instead, make it seem like you are the victim of his actions and you don't realize that you have been terribly wronged. Other people will become shocked and even outraged that he would do this to poor little innocent you. They may even become your soldiers, confronting him and making him feel guilty.

Guilt is your best trump card. Use it well. But also use it wisely. Playing the victim card too often will wear out its power.

Dr. Cialdini's Six Principles of Influence

You can use the Six Principles of Influence to influence any person to do what you want. These six principles are the foundation blocks of persuasion and manipulation. Keep them in mind and use them to gain influence over others. You can get what you want by using these principles.

The first principle is the reciprocity that we already discussed. Basically, you want to make people feel as if they owe you. Do favors for people so that you can call on them later when you need something. Appear very warm and generous so that others want to do things for you.

The second principle involves social proof. You basically want to be well-liked. The more popular you are, the more influence you have. Other people will back you up if you are well-liked. And new people that you meet will want to do things for you to gain your favor, since everyone else likes you.

Commitment and consistency is the third principle. People tend to stick to things that they know. They like consistency. So you can appeal to someone by asking him to do something that he already does. This works well in sales – if you have a customer who always likes the same types of products, you should target him with similar products. Brand loyalty is built upon this principle.

Authority grants you a lot of influence. If you appear like an authority figure, others will do what you say. The infamous Milton Prison Experiment is a classic example of how people are willing to obey authority figures to great lengths. Appear like you know what you are doing and be bossy. People will believe that you have more power than you really do if you act like it.

Scarcity is where you can essentially scare someone into action. Let your subject know that something is in limited supply. He will jump into action to get it before it runs out. This is the principle at play when TV commercials command you to act fast before supplies run out.

Liking is the final principle. This is where you want to make people like you. Being a kind, sincere person (at least on the outside) can make others want to do things for you. Also, appearing warm will make people like you. Approach someone with a proposal or favor in a warm room or offer him a warm drink to give the impression that you are warm. Use light touch, such as an arm brushing during conversation, and lots of eye contact to establish a bond. In Eastern cultures and some Native American cultures, eye contact and touch is not encouraged, so instead you want to appear deferent and deeply respectful at all times, keep your hands to yourself, and avoid eye contact.

Denial

Denial is extremely powerful. People don't want to believe things that hurt them. So they put up fronts and convince themselves that reality is just peachy. You can use denial to your favor when you are manipulating someone.

One way to use denial is to justify your own behavior to yourself. You won't be a great manipulator if you feel bad about what you're doing. You need to justify what you are doing to yourself. Denying the level of depravity that you have sunk to is a great way to do this.

Another thing that you can use denial for is manipulating your subject. Use his own sense of denial against him. Tell him that he is in denial about things to convince him that he is in the wrong. Make him think that you know him better than he knows himself. That will make him rely on you yet more for affirmation and validation of himself. It will also make him start to doubt himself and wonder what it is that he is in denial about.

Finally, denial is great for defending yourself. Vehemently deny any and all wrongdoing. Should someone accuse you of being less than upfront and trying to manipulate others, deny it. Never admit to any wrongdoing. You want to appear like you have done nothing wrong. This will make your subject believe it. If you stand steadfastly beside your innocence, you will appear more innocent. Eventually, your subject may cave and rethink his accusations. He may even stop suspecting you of any wrongdoing. Use this opportunity to convince him that he is just seeing things or being too sensitive or thinking of a past friend, lover, or family member who was manipulative to him. Tell him that he is projecting stuff onto you and that it isn't fair to you. Again, you want to whip out that victim card and even convince yourself that you are a victim. This makes the denial even more complete.

Chapter 5: Brainwash and Hypnotism

Hypnotism Is Real

Of all the aspects of dark psychology presented in this audiobook, hypnotism is the one most likely to raise eyebrows. When most people hear the word "hypnotism" they think of a guy with a moustache and a top hat waving a pocket watch while insisting someone is "getting very sleepy." Believing in this stereotype is actually dangerous. This is because real hypnotists are out there and are equipped with subtle but powerful techniques. These people are able to draw upon the darkest elements of psychology to influence people in an incredibly powerful way.

So if hypnotism isn't the old stereotypical image of a stage hypnotist, what exactly is hypnosis? Simply put, it is the ability to make suggestions to someone that filter through deep layers of their consciousness. This ability to make deep, impactful suggestions to someone while they are in a vulnerable and suggestible state grants hypnotic dark manipulators a high level of power over their victims. Unlike almost every other technique in this audiobook, hypnotism is not something that people encounter in a milder, more innocent form in their day-to-day lives.

Hypnotism can take the form of both verbal and nonverbal suggestive practices. Often, the forms of suggestion are very subtle and therefore difficult to detect. By its very nature, hypnosis works on the deepest levels of a person's mind. Someone who is skilled in generating a hypnotic state and response in someone will be able to bypass their defenses and influence them without raising any alarms or giving a person a chance to raise their guard.

Hypnotic Tactics

Now that you understand the difference between the stereotype of what hypnosis is, and what it actually is, it is time to explore the main hypnotic tactics. There are many variations on these types of tactics but they offer an insight into the main things to be wary of. Examples of how each tactic can be used will be provided wherever possible to give a clear insight into how hypnotists operate in our midst, undetected, every day.

Suggestion Can Be Silent

If hypnotism, in a darkly psychological sense of the word, can be understood as "deep suggestion," then it is important to understand what exactly is meant by suggestion in this instance. Most people might imagine a suggestion is a clearly stated statement like "I suggest you do this." This is far from the truth. The dark psychology view of suggestion is very far apart from the usual understanding of the word. The first important concept to grasp is the fact that hypnotic suggestion can be either verbal or nonverbal.

Picture the human brain as an iceberg. The part of the iceberg that is above the surface of the water represents the known and understood aspects of cognitive function such as thought. The larger, deeper part of the ice submerged below the water represents parts of the brain that are consciously inaccessible and little understood. If you doubt the power of this hidden portion of the brain you need only think of dreaming and the immense power of the mind to generate series of images, pictures, and sounds while a person is asleep. Dark hypnotists target their efforts toward this hidden, subconscious part of the mind.

There are, broadly speaking, two types of suggestion used by hypnotists—silent and verbal. Both types of hypnotic technique come in a variety of different forms. The exact type of hypnotism a manipulative person chooses to use at any given time depends on a range of factors. Some manipulators will carry out whichever form of hypnotism they feel will be most impactful on their victim's particular psyche. Others carry out whichever technique they happen to wish to use for their own amusement at the time. This depends largely on whether the hypnotist is seeking to exert influence in the most powerful way possible or is merely trying to control someone for their own fun and games.

Verbal suggestion is very difficult to detect. Sometimes, dark hypnotists are able to implant suggestions into their victim's mind using words that sound similar to other, more innocent words.

To take a deeply dark example, if a hypnotist was trying to instill suicidal feelings in their target, they may mask the true command of "You want to die" as something similar sounding such as "You want to dine." The hypnotist would speak the words "you want to die" clearly, but in a context that would mask the true content. For example, the hypnotist could talk about an upcoming trip and state "You have to check out the local restaurants, you want to die, somewhere that is popular but picturesque." The victim's mind would absorb the suggestion of death without consciously understanding why!

The above example of masked verbal suggestions is akin to a poison being hidden in someone's food. The victim consumes the hidden content, thinking that they are enjoying something helpful and innocuous when in actual fact they are absorbing something deadly. The especially devastating part of this technique is the fact the victim will never notice it. Even if someone thought they had picked up on the true words the hypnotist had spoken, imagine how crazy they would sound calling them out! People will generally take whichever option is psychologically easier for them and will therefore accept the masked command without question.

A hypnotist's tone of voice and choice of words is another method of verbal suggestion. Some hypnotists will carefully learn the pace and style of delivery a particular victim uses when they are expressing something serious.

For example, if, when someone wishes to say something meaningful, their voice lowers in pitch and slows in pace, the hypnotist would memorize this detail and retain it for future use. The hypnotist would then make suggestions to the victim in that exact, mirrored tone of voice. Because of the carefully modulated tone, the words delivered in that vocal variation would deeply penetrate a victim's defenses. Because the hypnotist would only deliver the suggestive content in that tone of voice, and then switch back to their usual way of speaking, the victim would be unaware even of what had taken place.

Another form of personalized, verbal suggestion employed by a hypnotic user of dark psychology is to pick up on words that have a special, intense significance for the victim who uses them. For example, when someone is very emotional they will often use a particular term to convey this feeling. If the hypnotic manipulator is able to pick up on these personal words then they are able to deploy them for their own benefit. Just as people have a specific tone of voice, they have a list of personal words of meaning, without often knowing it. The manipulator will understand their victim better than the victim understands herself. Knowing these words and tones, the manipulator can reverse engineer the victim's own brain to use against them.

Suggestion can also take nonverbal forms as well. This can be through the hypnotic manipulator's body language or even cues they place in their environment. If you think such seemingly trivial things could not exert a hypnotic influence then think again! Even political leaders have made use of such tactics in ways such as changing their hairstyle to convey a different intention during speeches. As discomforting as it is to believe, the human mind is deeply susceptible to even the smallest hints and cues.

So what are some of the main ways a hypnotic manipulator can use nonverbal suggestion against their victim? The technique centers around the idea of association. A skilled hypnotist is able to consistently link a strong emotion to some kind of external stimulus such as a particular eye movement they use. For example, if a hypnotist wanted to be able to trigger a feeling of panic in a victim, they may choose to make a particular motion with their eyes whenever the victim was thinking about, or experiencing, panic. The victim's subconscious would then learn to link the eye movement to the feeling. Over time, the hypnotist would be able to trigger the emotional response simply by making the eye movement, even without the need for any other stimulus.

Environmental stimulus is another form of nonverbal suggestion that forms a part of the hypnotist's toolkit. Think of environmental stimulus as like being summoned to the principal's office as a child. The location itself was enough to send you into a feeling of deep panic because you had learned to associate the location with panic and problems. Hypnotists are able to use this same concept to devastating effect in adult life.

For example, they will often be sure to have a certain type of conversation with a victim in one location only. Picture a hypnotist and their victim in a romantic relationship. Every time the hypnotist wishes to get some kind of agreement or consent from his victim, he may be sure to ask her only when they are at a certain coffee shop. Over a period of time, the victim's mind begins to associate the physical environment of the coffee shop with the granting of permission. The hypnotist can then use this physical environment as external psychological leverage whenever he needs to exert influence and control.

Vulnerable Victims

Hypnotism is not equally effective on everybody it is tried on. Some people are more likely to be influenced by a hypnotist than others. Although the exact level of susceptibility is complex and hard to simplify in a single sentence, it boils down to the idea of vulnerability. Vulnerable people are more likely to be agreeable to hypnotic suggestion than people who are less vulnerable. The types of vulnerability sought out by hypnotists in their victims will now be explored along with a guide to how hypnotists exacerbate and magnify the vulnerable paradigm.

The people most vulnerable to hypnotism are those who have recently experienced a significant life-changing event that has reduced their stability and certainty. For example, if a person has just come out of a serious romantic relationship, has suffered bereavement or lost their job, they are particularly vulnerable to suggestion. This is because the human brain craves certainty and understanding above all else. If a hypnotist spots someone who is in a vulnerable place they can offer them certainty and change their vulnerability in general to vulnerability around the hypnotist specifically.

There are roughly two facets of vulnerability in a hypnotist's victim—preexisting vulnerability and exacerbated vulnerability. The most diabolical hypnotists are able to combine both aspects to lethal effect. Not only will the best hypnotic manipulators be able to find someone who is suitably vulnerable, they will find someone who is specifically vulnerable to the hypnotic psychological scheme they have planned.

For example, if a hypnotist is looking to use their powers to gain financially, they might seek out a victim such as a rich, recently bereaved widow. They will then, subtly and over time, associate their own self with feelings of security and comfort while increasing the widow's general feelings of loss and vulnerability. Eventually, the hypnotist is the victim's only refuge from a hell of their own making.

As well as seeking out vulnerability in general, hypnotists are known to seek out situational vulnerability as well. This is when someone is in a situational circumstance that makes them more suggestible than their overall "baseline" of suggestibility. There are tactical tricks a hypnotist can use to ascertain this situational vulnerability. One such tactic is trying to induce "mirroring" behavior in their target. When people feel a subconscious level of connection and rapport with someone they will start to "mirror" the person without knowing they are doing it. To check this, a hypnotist might make some small change to their body language, such as a hand motion. If the victim subconsciously mimics this gesture, then it is a sign the victim is situationally vulnerable.

Now that both general and situational vulnerability have been explored, it is important to understand how the most skilled hypnotists use the two types of vulnerability together for an especially strong impact. If someone is vulnerable in general, due to their life situation, and vulnerable in particular, due to the situation the hypnotist has managed to set up, then that person is in the most influenceable state imaginable. Once such a state has been induced the hypnotist is likely to move on to the most powerful and advanced techniques they possess, such as NLP.

NLP

NLP, or neurolinguistic programming, is a technique that is powerful even in the hands of the most well-intentioned people. Leaders within the world of business and philanthropy are some of the most common advocates of the techniques and principles offered by NLP. Placing such techniques in the hands of people willing to use dark psychology to exploit others is like giving a nuclear weapon to a psychopath. They possess both the power and the will to create serious psychological havoc among their victims. Understanding the main techniques used by practitioners of dark psychology offers insight into the way they can be deployed to devastating impact.

Anchoring

Anchoring is an NLP technique that involves linking an emotional state to some form of external stimulus. If you are familiar with the idea of Pavlovian conditioning, then you will understand this tactic. Hypnotists are able to induce a powerful emotion in a victim and then link it to a stimulus such as a physical gesture or tone of voice. The hypnotist is then able to induce this emotional state at will by performing the linked stimulus.

The most nefarious hypnotists will use the principle of anchoring in a very subtle and underhand way. They will work for a prolonged period of time to induce a variety of different anchors in the psyche of their victim without the victim's conscious awareness of what is taking place. This provides the manipulator with a set of hypnotic puppet strings that they can pull as and when they desire. Often, hypnotists will use an "anchor stack" to induce different intense feelings in quick succession. For example, they will induce the feeling of love, followed by terror, followed by love once more, all in quick succession. This series of emotions overloads the victim's emotional circuitry and leaves them as mere clay in the hands of their controller.

Reframing

Reframing is the art of controlling the way ambiguous information is perceived. There is an old saying that "nothing is good or bad unless we believe it to be." Reframing is the ultimate technique related to this idea. Hypnotists can use reframing to effectively control the way their victim thinks and feels. Think of a skilled reframer as an editor. They are able to selectively choose the victim's focus and the feelings the focus triggers. This is effectively hypnotic mind control.

So how does darkly psychological reframing work in practice? Let's take a situation where a hypnotic manipulator has influenced a victim to no longer spend time around, or communicating with, a particular person. The victim may state feelings of sadness or loss related to this interpersonal change. The hypnotist would be able to reframe these feelings into ones which suited the hypnotist's own purposes. This is best illustrated through an example dialogue.

Victim - "It sucks I haven't spoken to Rachel as much, I miss her."

Hypnotist - "I know you might hate how things are with Rachel, but I know you're smart enough to love the freedom you have now."

Notice how the concept of hate is linked to Rachel and love is linked to the "freedom" of being without her? The hypnotist also plays on the victim's ego by linking the idea of their intelligence to going along with the way the hypnotist wants them to perceive the "frame," or perception, of the facts. Think about what you have already learned about the vulnerability of victims and you will understand how this reframing can be used to devastating impact.

Future Pacing

Future pacing is the closest thing possible to psychologically manipulative time travel. Future pacing allows a skilled manipulator to lead their victim on a mental journey into the future and influence behaviors and responses that will occur in the actual, chronological future that exists independent of the victim's reality.

At its most fundamental, future pacing involves the mental leading of a victim through a future scenario. For example, if the hypnotist wants their victim to feel generous and relaxed whenever they receive money, the hypnotist would ask their victim to envision a situation, such as receiving their next paycheck. To make this future imagining possible the hypnotist would ensure the victim imagined all of their five senses in action—what they would see, feel, touch etc. at the time. This helps the brain to perceive the future scenario as "real" due to its sensory depth.

Once the hypnotist cognitively transports their victim into the future, they begin to suggest certain happenings and monitor the responses. For example, the hypnotist may say something like "Imagine being very generous with this paycheck and providing it to those who really need it, because you are a kind person and doing the right thing is deep in your nature." If the victim's physical response to this future scenario showed signs of compliance and acceptance then the hypnotic manipulator would have the confidence that their victim would actually behave in this way when the scenario occurs in the future.

Due to the intensity and power of the hypnotic techniques mentioned in this chapter, the best manipulators only use them in moderation. For example, a darkly psychological hypnotist would be sure to keep their interaction with a victim 95% normal. This will increase the victim's comfort and trust to such high levels that the 5% time spent on hypnotic influence would not only slip past a victim's defenses unnoticed but would work to great effect once embedded in the victim's mind.

Brainwashing

Are You Brainwashed About Brainwashing?

If you ask someone if they know what brainwashing is, they will probably reply that they do. Brainwashing is a concept that many people have heard of, while mistaking their vague familiarity for accurate understanding. Before looking at how, where, and why brainwashing occurs, it is essential to understand exactly what brainwashing is and isn't. Of all the dark psychology techniques contained in this audiobook, brainwashing has the most serious and widest impact. If the other dark psychology techniques are sniper bullets, aimed at one particular person, brainwashing is a nuclear bomb capable of devastating an entire city.

The term brainwashing refers to the slow process of replacing a person's ideas about identity and belief with new ideas that are intended to suit the purpose of the person doing the brainwashing. Brainwashing can occur in both wider and narrower contexts. For example, a brainwasher is able to control one person in particular, or use the same techniques and principles to control the minds of a wider group at once. Brainwashing is the process that turns atheists into suicide bombers and prisoners of war into communists. It has been tried, tested, and proven over the years to be effective in almost any scenario.

So what are the most common misunderstandings related to brainwashing? Many people picture the process as some kind of quick and forced occurrence. Picture either Alex in "A Clockwork Orange" or Neo in "The Matrix" having concepts forced into their cranium, involuntarily, in a short space of time. This is Hollywood brainwashing and is far from what actually occurs in real life.

The process of real-world brainwashing will be explored in detail later in this chapter, but at its simplest, brainwashing is a process involving the slow, gradual, and seemingly voluntary changing of a person's "map of reality" from the one they have freely put together to one that is forced upon them by the brainwasher. The evil irony of the technique is the brainwasher will ensure the victim feels in control at all times.

Brainwashing Contexts

So what are some of the main situations that are fertile breeding grounds for brainwashers? Before the process of brainwashing itself is explored fully, let's take a look at the situations in which people are often brainwashed and the motivations behind this.

A lot of people would agree with the idea that "cults brainwash people" but few would be able to explain exactly what a cult is and how they brainwash their recruits. Let's demystify the process. A cult is a fringe group, often built around a charismatic leader who is able to exert high levels of influence over their followers. The cult will usually provide a "complete understanding of reality" to those who follow it. Why exactly is this cult context one in which brainwashing flourishes?

The primary attraction of cults is they present reality as something very simple and within reach of the average person, provided the person is willing to take on board the cult's teachings. We live in a complex modern world where life can seem confusing and overwhelming. Cults cut through this confusion and tell people "don't worry, we have the answer." The way in which this "answer" is presented is intended to play on the human need for belonging and acceptance. Brainwashing can flourish in this context as a result of the idea of the "new normal."

What exactly is "the new normal"? It is a way in which cults are able to influence those they brainwash into accepting their teachings by making them seem prevalent, accepted and positive. For example, the idea of worshipping a man who claims to be God would be incredibly strange in everyday life. Within the closed environment of a cult, however, this behavior becomes "normal" to the extent that not doing it would seem strange to people within the cult! This process of persistent, social reinforcement is one of the most powerful ways in which the ideological brainwashing of cults is able to occur.

Think of cults as drug dealers. Perhaps the newcomer to the cult had been seeking something in their life and came across the cult, just as newcomers to the world of drugs often, misguidedly, seek out their first high of their own volition. The cult doesn't need to "push" the drug of their ideology onto the victim as the victim was already seeking the fulfillment of a void in their life. It is this initial "search" and "readiness" on the part of the people who are later brainwashed that makes them so susceptible to the brainwashing process itself.

Ideologies are another context, similar to cults, in which brainwashing is commonplace. The difference between a cult and an ideology is the focus of the ideology is on the idea itself rather than the person delivering the message and those who follow them. Whereas cults brainwash people into placing faith and trust in the cult leader and their followers, ideological brainwashing involves leading people to place absolute trust in an idea.

Ideological brainwashing is incredibly dangerous due to the fact it goes above and beyond any one individual. Think of extremist religious terrorism, for example. It is possible for a high profile figure within the ideology, such as Osama Bin Laden, to be killed. Does this kill support for the idea itself? No! The dead figures are praised as martyrs who gave their life to the ideology, thus increasing its attractiveness and allure to potential newcomers.

Almost any ideology is likely to have an extremist, fringe outskirt in which brainwashing takes place. Even something seemingly innocent like a pop band can have this impact. Young fans, at a psychologically impressionable age, link their sense of identity, happiness, and belonging to a pop group. They will gladly defend this group to extents that are unusually intense. Some pop groups have fans that even self-harm, using razor blades, if a member quits the group! If you carefully consider this phenomenon of the power of brainwashing even in accidental, innocent contexts, then consider how devastating the process can be in intended contexts like cults and terrorist groups.

Now that you have a clear understanding of the way brainwashing can occur in broader social contexts, such as cults and ideologies, it is important to understand that a personal, one-on-one context is also a ripe situation for elements of brainwashing to occur in. There are similarities and differences between "group" and "individual" brainwashing and understanding these nuances can help to identify when either type is occurring.

Personal brainwashing is similar to group brainwashing as it involves the slow and steady replacement of existing beliefs with new beliefs that serve the objectives of the brainwasher. Instead of relying on group dynamics to reinforce "the new normal," a one on one brainwashing situation will instead rely on a deep, personal connection between the brainwasher and the victim. This can be even more powerful than group brainwashing as the content can be modified and altered to the particular psychological constitution of the victim.

The Process Of Brainwashing

Now that you understand the reality of what brainwashing is, and where it occurs, let's take a look at the specific process itself. Distinctions will be drawn between the way in which the process applies to both group and individual situations.

The starting point of any episode of brainwashing is the mental state and social circumstance of the victim. This is the foundation upon which the rest of the process is entirely reliant. Brainwashing is not something that can be carried out on absolutely anyone. It requires the identification of a person who is seeking something or trying to fill a void in their life.

So what kind of people are ideal victims for brainwashers? People who have had their existing reality shaken up by a recent event are prime targets for brainwashers. For example, many of the Western men who have travelled to become terrorists in Syria, and detonate suicide bombs, have done so after the death of a close friend or relative. When their existing world loses its meaning and certainty, brainwashers can step in and provide that certainty in the form of a murderous ideology.

Once a brainwashing victim has been identified, either in person or via the Internet, the actual process of brainwashing begins. Contrary to the popular image of a brainwasher as a wide-eyed psychopath who will incessantly and angrily indoctrinate their victim, real-world brainwashers are anything but this. They will come across as calm, friendly, rational people who have their lives together in a way the victim does not. Imagine being homeless and being befriended by a celebrity. This is how the process of meeting their brainwasher for the first time feels for a victim.

The brainwasher will often work initially on creating a level of trust and rapport between themselves and their victim. This usually involves creating both deep and superficial similarities. For example, superficial similarities may involve surface level preferences like an enjoyment of the same sport or even food! Deeper level rapport may involve some "deep" shared experience in the past of both the brainwasher and the victim. Brainwashers will convincingly fake these if needed. If the victim shares the fact that they have lost a relative in the past, guess what? The brainwasher suddenly has a similar story to tell.

The false emotional warmth and connection explained above is not the only aspect of brainwashing that occurs initially. The brainwasher will often provide gifts and other favors to their victim. For example, the brainwasher may treat them to meals or send them gadgets or other useful items. This creates a sense of gratitude and indebtedness from the victim to their brainwasher and softens up any resistance the victim may initially experience.

One of the most powerful examples of the above initial kindness can be taken from Prisoner of War camps. When American troops have been captured in the past, their captors often offer them American cigarettes and speak to them in a respectful way. This reverses the expectations of the victim and opens the victim's mind to the further brainwashing process that is to follow.

A utopian presentation is the next step in the brainwashing process, following the initial victim identification and rapport building stages. This involves the brainwasher slowly and increasingly offering a solution to all of the problems that the victim has opened up about. This is always done in a casual, offhand way at first to avoid any negative experiences of pressure the victim may experience otherwise. This utopian solution is always whatever cult, ideology or personality the brainwasher is trying to convert their victim to— terrorism, communism or just a charismatic brainwasher's own need for validation and praise.

When performed correctly, the initial stages of this process will leave a victim craving more and more information and understanding of the solution that is being hinted at. The brainwasher may even withhold this information initially, as if it is something that the victim must work at being worthy of attaining. This will lead to a strong motivation on behalf of the victim to seek out and accept the information they are eventually provided with. Thanks to the preceding steps, the poisonous ideas that are being implanted into the victim will seem as natural and refreshing as cold water on a hot day.

Once the victim is being spoon fed snippets of their new belief system, and responding well to them, the brainwasher will be very careful to reveal the right things at the right time. This is a concept that is sometimes known as "milk before meat" or "gradual revelation." It basically involves the presentation of easy to accept ideas before anything controversial is revealed. For example, in the case of religious terrorism, recruiters may initially focus on convincing their victim that God loves them. This is usually quite acceptable. More objectionable ideas, such as God wants you to blow yourself up, are saved until far further down the line. At this point, the brainwashing has reached the point of no return.

You may be questioning way a victim continues to engage with their brainwasher once the objectionable ideas begin to become apparent.

The reason is threefold. First, the already vulnerable victim now feels a strong sense of liking and approval of their brainwasher.

Second, the victim has invested time and sometimes money into the process thus far. This is known as the "sunk cost fallacy." The victim is loath to "throw away all their hard work" by walking away from the process.

Finally, the brainwasher is likely to have amassed a lot of secretive and sensitive information on their victim. This "dirt" can then be held over the victim's head, either discreetly or overtly.

Both the ideas of a vulnerable victim and the "sunk cost fallacy" make logical sense. The idea of blackmail and control may be harder to understand at first. Why would a victim respond well to such threats? Well, they are rarely presented in a threatening way. For example, if the victim has divulged a lot of sensitive information to a brainwasher, and then begins to give signs of walking away, the brainwasher may appear concerned and insist that "if I can't help you anymore with your problems, I need to make sure someone else can. Perhaps your family or boss need to know what's been going on with you, so they can look out for you when I'm not there."

Because of the deep sense of rapport and warmth the brainwasher has manipulated their victim into feeling, the above form of blackmail and control is often actually perceived as kind, compassionate behavior. It is often enough to make the victim see "sense" and agree to remain on the brainwashing path they have embarked upon. Brainwashers are adept at making the pain and struggle of walking away seem epic, so staying becomes the preferable, easy option by default.

The end product of this process is the victim believing everything they have been indoctrinated to view as the truth. The power of the process is that the victim will feel they have chosen these views as their own and have sought them out through their own volition. This leaves a previously normal individual as an indoctrinated psychological slave to something they have no idea even exists.

The Impact Of Brainwashing

The above analysis of the brainwashing process shows the severity and depth of the technique. It is inevitable that a process as powerful as this has lasting consequences. Some of the main impacts of brainwashing after the process has been completed will now be explored.

Loss of identity is one of the most serious side effects of brainwashing. A feature of many cults and ideologies is that people who complete their initiation process are given a new name. This allows the person's psyche to totally detach from their old identity. They can believe things and do things they would never have done before as the person they used to be no longer exists. When carried out carefully the brainwashing process leaves a victim feeling as if their old identity was no more real or permanent than a nightmare from which they have awoken.

So is brainwashing simply a process of ideas? Not at all. If brainwashing resulted in only the change of opinions then it would be far less of a problem than it actually is. The main danger of brainwashing is it not only changes the ways that people think and feel but also the way they behave. People go from functional members of the society with acceptable, positive jobs and interests to brainwashed zombies willing to carry out rape, murder, and suicide. This sounds sensational and dramatic, but it's true. Read on for the proof.

If you have any doubts about what brainwashing can drive a person to, consider the following examples. Members of some religious cults will gladly cut off all contact from their family, leave their careers behind, surrender all their wealth and possessions, and place their autonomy entirely in the hands of the organization that has brainwashed them. This is not all. The victim will see their new lifestyle as a blessing they are fortunate to have, rather than something unpleasant they have been forced into.

Another example of the toxic outcome of brainwashing is the repeated tale of young people becoming brainwashed by religious extremists to travel to a foreign land and drive a car packed full of explosives into a group of people they have never met and who have never hurt them. Such young victims are often educated people with a track record of success in life and a family history free of turmoil or abuse. These tragic losses of life are testament to the overwhelming, all-conquering power of the brainwashing process.

PTSD (post traumatic stress disorder) is another hallmark of those who manage to escape, or are rescued from, a situation of intense brainwashing. Brainwashing victims often show the same physical and psychological signs as war veterans who have witnessed their friends being blown apart next to them during combat. The severity of this traumatic aftermath shows that a brainwashing situation can harm a person as much as a world war.

Perhaps the most shocking examples of the long-term impact of brainwashing are the numerous instances of people who have been rescued or escaped from a brainwashing situation, only to later return of their own free will. Even once they are outside of the controlling, brainwashing environment, the legacy of the process runs so deep through a person's mind, they seek to return to it. This is a form of Stockholm syndrome. The escapees will actually praise their brainwashers far into the future and defend, support, and justify the ideological stances they were indoctrinated with while captive.

Conclusion

Time to take a deep breath and assimilate all the information presented to you, in this book.

If you are experiencing a stressful time, it can be useful to learn relaxation techniques. They will help you manage your mental wellbeing. Many of these can be done in the privacy of your own home, or even in a work situation.

Your mental wellbeing is as important as your physical health. It plays an important role in your happiness. You owe it to yourself to break out of any unhealthy stronghold that others might place on you, such as a manipulative character. No one could be happy living or working alongside another person who belittles them. Most particularly if that person coerces them into doing something they don't want to do. That is exactly what living with a controlling person is like, at work or home. You will feel trapped as they slowly destroy your self-esteem. If your partner or work colleague is never open to compromise, then they may well be manipulative and controlling. A healthy relationship, be it personal or work related, should be one whereby everyone feels comfortable.

Most of us grow up to be taught the social rules of good manners and acceptable behavior. Unfortunately, some either ignore this learning process or have no one to teach and guide them. We need positive role models in our informative years. Those who may have suffered abuse either physically or mentally as children, will be scarred in some form or another. Many will still manage a normal life, but it's unlikely that anyone can come out of a bad childhood unscathed.

Many of us struggle on in our daily lives. We perform routine tasks to make our lives pleasant and our loved ones happy. There comes a time when we do not always have the energy or inclination to help other people. Most of us will do a kindness along the way. Always though, our priorities are for our own loved ones. There is a certain necessity to be strong if you wish to make something of your life. Otherwise, depression can set in and you may drown in the many temptations around you. Excessive eating, or even worse the temptations of alcohol and drugs could seem an easy way out.

It does take courage to stand up to a controlling manipulative character, but you must be brave and see it through. Push them away from your life and keep them at arm's length. Don't be taken in by their false promises. If someone encompasses you so tightly that you feel you cannot breathe, then you must escape. A healthy relationship should not feel like that.

This book should enlighten you on how to cope with some of the problems you may face in life. It is meant only as a guide on how to deal with controlling manipulative relationships. It cannot give you your freedom. Only courage can do that. Build up your self-confidence. Take care of your health. For the sake of living a happy life, learn how to handle such controlling characters that may pass you by.

Thank you.

www.ingramcontent.com/pod-product-compliance
Lightning Source LLC
Chambersburg PA
CBHW021130080526
44587CB00012B/1224